W9-CEY-882

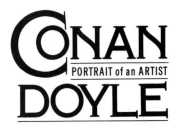

CONAN
PORTRAIT of an ARTIST
DOYLE

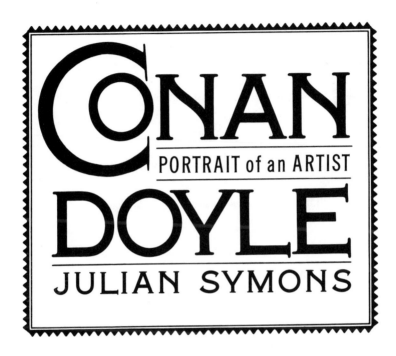

CONAN
PORTRAIT of an ARTIST
DOYLE
JULIAN SYMONS

THE MYSTERIOUS PRESS

New York • London • Tokyo

Originally published by G. Whizzard, London

Copyright © 1979 by Julian Symons
All rights reserved.
The Mysterious Press, 129 West 56th Street, New York, N.Y. 10019

This Mysterious Press edition is published by arrangement with
the author

Printed in the United States of America
First Mysterious Press Trade Paperback Printing: November 1988
10 9 8 7 6 5 4 3 2 1

Library of Congress Cataloging-In-Publication Data
Symons, Julian, 1912 -
    Conan Doyle, portrait of an artist.

    Reprint. Originally published: London: G. Whizzard,
1979.
    Bibliography p.
    Includes index.
    1. Doyle, Arthur Conan, Sir, 1859-1930. 2. Authors,
English—20th century—Biography, I. Title
PR4623.S9   1987   823'.8 [B]   87.20432
ISBN 0-89296-926-1 (pbk.) (U.S.A.)
        0-89296-927-X (pbk.) (Canada)

CONTENTS

AUTHOR'S NOTE

To write a new biography of Sir Arthur Conan Doyle when several books about him are already on library shelves may seem to need an excuse, and an attempt to compass his varied life within only one hundred or so pages, and to include some critical observations on his work in that small space, may seem both presumptuous and foolhardy. I can only say that there seemed to me room for a short study which looked at the life rather differently from the way it is generally seen to-day, and tried to sum up his achievement for a new generation. If another reason is necessary, it would lie in my belief that for some time now we have heard perhaps too much about Sherlock Holmes, and certainly too little about the other achievements of his creator. I finished writing the book—and this is not something a biographer can always say—with more admiration for its subject than when I began it.

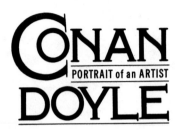

CONAN
PORTRAIT of an ARTIST
DOYLE

Conan Doyle in his study, round about the time he began to make a name for himself as a writer.

CHAPTER ONE
THE CREATOR OF SHERLOCK HOLMES

Early in 1886 a young and not very successful doctor, living in a suburb of Portsmouth called Southsea, jotted down some notes about a story he proposed to write, and about the characters. He put down as a title "A tangled skein", crossed it out and replaced it by "A Study in Scarlet". What about the names of the characters? "Ormond Sacker", Arthur Conan Doyle wrote, "from Afghanistan". Ormond Sacker lived at 221B Upper Baker Street with Sherrinford Holmes, who was put down as "reserved—sleepy eyed young man—philosopher—collector of rare Violins". With Sherrinford changed to Sherlock, and Ormond Sacker replaced by Dr John H. Watson, Conan Doyle sat down and wrote the story. One of the most powerful and enduring myths in English literature had been born, a myth so powerful that it has almost swamped its creator. If you stopped a hundred people in the street, it is likely that no more than half of them would be able to identify Conan Doyle, but in the literate world Sherlock Holmes is truly a universal name.

The author had difficulty in finding a publisher for the booklet, as he called it, and at last sold it for the miserable sum of £25 outright. The publishers told him at the time that they "could not publish it this year as the market is flooded at present by cheap fiction". It remained largely

Baker Street in Sherlock Holmes' day.

The Sherlock Holmes Room on permanent display in the 'Sherlock Holmes' pub in London leaves little doubt as to the occupant.

unnoticed, although an American publisher asked for another Sherlock Holmes novel, and *The Sign of the Four* was written for him. This also attracted no particular attention. Between April and August, 1891, however, Conan Doyle wrote six Sherlock Holmes short stories, and these were immediately accepted by the recently-founded *Strand Magazine*, at the quite handsome fee of £35 apiece. Conan Doyle meant to write only those six, because he thought of himself as a serious novelist and Holmes, as he told his mother, "takes my mind from better things". When the *Strand* wanted more, he asked for £50 a story, and they agreed at once to pay that amount.

So the Sherlock Holmes saga began. The slightly reluctant author was pulled along in the wake of the amazing success of the short stories, which quickly made him famous throughout the English-speaking world. At the end of a second series he sent Holmes to his death over Reichenbach Falls, locked in the embrace of Professor Moriarty. Doyle felt a great sense of relief. As he wrote to a friend:

> I have had such an overdose of him that I feel towards him as I do towards *pâté de foie gras*, of which I once ate too much, so that the name of it gives me a sickly feeling to this day.

Holmes did not return for eight years, and when he did, in *The Hound of the Baskervilles*, it was made clear that this was an early adventure. It was not until Conan Doyle received in 1903 an offer from America of $5000 a story, with, in addition, a fee of £100 a thousand words from the *Strand*, that he capitulated and wrote the first story of a new series, "The Empty House", about Holmes's return. Having once given way he made no further attempt to abandon Holmes, although he agreed with the critic who said that the detective had never been quite the same man after he came back from the Reichenbach Falls. He wrote in all four Sherlock Holmes novels and five collections of short stories.

The enduring power of the Sherlock Holmes myth is astonishing. When the 1951 Festival of Britain was being planned, the borough of St Marylebone decided, after some hesitation, to include a reconstruction of the Baker Street sitting room as an exhibit. As soon as the idea became known masses of period relics were sent in, among them violins, magnifying glasses, meerschaum pipes, deer-stalker hats and old newspapers. Along with these came relics of many famous cases, like the footprints of the hound of the Baskervilles and letters from grateful clients with the proper period date stamps on them. The exhibition was a great success, and the room can still be seen in London's "Sherlock Holmes" pub. A railway train has been named for him. Many parodies of the detective and his methods have been produced. In a few of them he has gone by his own name, but mostly he has masqueraded as Herlock Sholmes, Holmlock Shears, Shylock Homes, Shamrock Johnes, Sherlaw Kombs, Schlock Homes—the list could be lengthened.

There are Sherlock Holmes Societies in almost every country, with names like Silver Blazers and Baker Street Irregulars which refer to the stories. The British Sherlock Holmes Society, founded in 1934, has organized a trip to the Reichenbach Falls, where the famous struggle was re-enacted in Victorian dress. At least four biographies of Holmes have been written, and there are a hundred collections of essays about various aspects of the saga, all of them based upon the supposition that Holmes and Watson were real people, and Conan Doyle merely their inaccurate recorder. In the last few years there has been a spate of novels, among which Nicholas Meyer's *The Seven Per Cent Solution* is the most amusing, although not the most accurate.

Plays and films have kept the fire of the saga well stoked. In 1897 Conan Doyle wrote a play called *Sherlock Holmes* and sent it to the famous actor-manager Beerbohm Tree, who wanted the central character's part rewritten and much changed. Conan Doyle had enough feeling for Holmes to refuse to do this, saying that it might be better to put the play back in the drawer. However, it was sold by the author's agent to the American actor William Gillette, who resembled the drawings of Holmes made by the artist Sidney Paget so remarkably that first sight of him took Conan Doyle's breath away. Conan Doyle had already told the actor that he could murder or marry Holmes. Now, enchanted by Gillette's appearance and manner, Doyle approved of the American's revisions to the original script, and said that he had written a fine play. It was certainly an immensely successful one, both in the United States and Britain, and

Sherlock Holmes plunging to his death
over the Reichenbach Falls with the
infamous Moriarty, as told in 'The
Final Problem'.

Gillette's aquiline features and deep-set eyes set a pattern for many representations of Holmes in theatre and cinema. When the English actor John Wood played Holmes in an up-dated version of Gillette's play, he worked out that he was the hundred and ninth actor to play the part in theatre and cinema.

Most of the plays and films bear little resemblance to the stories, except in their two principal characters Holmes and Watson, although "The Speckled Band", which was adapted for the stage by the author himself, provides an exception, as do some of the early films in which Eille Norwood played Holmes. But more recent films have shown Holmes foiling Moriarty's plans to get hold of a new bombsight, guarding the heir to the throne of Rovenia, meeting Jack the Ripper, and (in the film of Meyer's novel) solving a mystery with the help of Sigmund Freud. Many of these stories are quite outside the Doyle canon, in which no story takes place after 1914, since they make the assumption that the detective is alive and active in the modern world. They emphasize the lasting quality of the

Poster for the play 'Sherlock Holmes', featuring the American actor William Gillette in the title role.

Portrait of Dr Joseph Bell on whom Conan Doyle based the character of Sherlock Holmes.

Holmes myth, and its power of adaptation from one period to another.

The thing that most astonished and delighted early readers of the stories was Holmes's deductive skill, the way in which he was able to deduce a man's occupation by looking at him, and even to read Watson's thoughts through the direction of his gaze and the changing expressions on his face. Conan Doyle always said that the model for these deductive skills was Dr Joseph Bell, surgeon at Edinburgh Infirmary, and one of the professors at Edinburgh University when Conan Doyle was a medical student. Bell took a fancy to the young student, and appointed Conan Doyle as his outpatient clerk. In appearance Bell was thin and dark, with piercing grey eyes and a narrow aquiline nose, so that he had some resemblance to the imagined Sherlock Holmes. In his approach he was, if Conan Doyle is to be believed, identical. As a new case was brought into the room he would say: "This man is a left-handed cobbler", and then explain: "You'll observe, gentlemen, the worn places on the corduroy breeches where a cobbler rests his lapstone? The right-hand side, you'll note, is far more worn than the left. He uses his left hand for hammering the leather." This was one among many similar deductions made by Dr Bell. The young student was greatly impressed, and a few years later scrawled in one of his notebooks: "The coat-sleeves, the trouser-knee, the callosities of the forefinger and thumb—any one of these might tell us, but that all united should fail to enlighten the trained observation is incredible."

He used the Bell deductive approach when he began to write the stories.

It can be found in the deductions made from a battered old felt hat in "The Blue Carbuncle", the way in which Sherlock and his brother Mycroft cap each other's observations in "The Greek Interpreter", and the deduction in "The Red-Headed League" which is based partly upon the appearance of a suspect's trousers. Some of the clues would bear other interpretations than those given them (Dr Bell modestly said that Conan Doyle had exaggerated his powers), but that does not matter. The dazzling cleverness of Holmes is genuine, and although his approach has often been imitated, the effects he achieved have never been matched.

The American writer Edgar Allan Poe whose stories influenced Doyle.

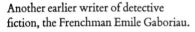

Another earlier writer of detective fiction, the Frenchman Emile Gaboriau.

Eugène François Vidoçq, former criminal who became first chief of the Sûreté.

But Dr Bell was not the author's only influence. He took something from earlier writers of detective stories. Holmes's ability to read Watson's thoughts is taken from Edgar Allan Poe's "Murders in the Rue Morgue", written half a century earlier, in which the detective Dupin does just the same thing. The French novelist Emile Gaboriau was the first to give an account of making plaster casts of footprints, and to show that a clock or watch may be set to give a deliberately misleading clue. Nor was the Holmes-Watson relationship unique. Both Poe and Gaboriau had given their detectives less intelligent friends or police colleagues, so that their own powers would shine more brightly. Holmes's skill in disguise is derived from Eugène François Vidoçq, the former criminal who in 1811 became the first chief of the Sûreté, and was said to have stained his face with walnut liquor, and to have painted mock blisters and fetter marks on his legs when impersonating an ex-convict. Conan Doyle acknowledged his debts, particularly to Poe, but like Shakespeare he transformed everything he borrowed.

Sherlock Holmes remains the supreme fictional detective of all time.

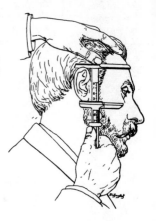

Measuring the right ear. Part of the Alphonse Bertillon method for establishing individual identification, used by many police forces in the late 19th century.

In part this is attributable to the period in which he first flowered, in part to Conan Doyle's talents as writer and storyteller. When the short stories began to appear there was no fingerprint system, Lombroso's views about the existence of a criminal type which could be discovered through careful measurements of various parts of the body (in particular the forehead and ears) was generally accepted, and the anthropometric methods of Alphonse Bertillon, which were based on the idea that by taking a sufficient number of physical measurements you could establish individual identification, was the most scientific approach used by enlightened police forces. The Bertillon method, which also involved a new method of criminal photography called the *portrait parlé*, was adopted throughout Europe during the eighteen nineties, except in Britain. It was dealt a death blow when an innocent man proved to have identical Bertillon measurements with a criminal. Scotland Yard no doubt congratulated themselves that they had not adopted anthropometry. In 1900 Britain was in the vanguard of countries using fingerprints as the official system of criminal identification, but it was several years before this newfangled idea was fully accepted by police forces.

It is important to understand this background. Inspector Lestrade, probably the most obtuse of the official detectives in the Holmes stories, is typical and not exceptional in his crude rejection of anything resembling intellectual reasoning or smacking of scientific method. The usual plain-clothes detective of the time was a man of little education, a thief-taker who relied upon his knowledge of underworld habits and characters for success. Yet the general Victorian reverence for science was strong, so that a detective who claimed that he approached criminal cases by scientific methods had an audience waiting for him. The references in the Holmes stories to his monograph on a hundred and forty varieties of pipe, cigar and cigarette tobaccos, his ability to make chemical analyses and to recognize different newspaper types at a glance, all helped to assure readers that Sherlock Holmes was a truly exceptional man.

Conan Doyle had a clear picture in his mind of the detective's appearance. He was very tall, over six feet but looking much taller because he was so thin. The face was thin and razor-like, "with a great hawk's-bill of a nose, and two small eyes, set close together on either side of it." When Sidney Paget was commissioned to draw the Holmes now fixed in our memory, however, he used his brother Walter as a model, and as Doyle put it, "the handsome Walter took the place of the more powerful

"HOLMES GAVE ME A SKETCH OF THE EVENTS."

Sidney Paget illustration from 'Silver Blaze' in *Strand Magazine*.

A kerchief design of the actress Lola Montes, on whom Conan Doyle is thought to have based the character Irene Adler in 'A Scandal in Bohemia'.

but uglier Sherlock." If Conan Doyle's original conception had been fully realized we should have had a character tougher and less intellectual in appearance. It was the combination in Holmes of the great thinker with the man of action that appealed to his first readers, near the end of the nineteenth century. Their own lives were humdrum and intensely respectable. They longed for romance and excitement, and found them in the Holmes stories, together with the reassuring thought that one of the great intellects of the world was on their side, opposed to the forces of crime.

Sherlock Holmes thus appeared as the great protector of bourgeois society, and he was made more attractive by the fact that his personal life in some respects outraged bourgeois standards. Holmes was unmarried, and "never spoke of the softer passions, save with a gibe and a sneer", although women found him sympathetic and he nursed some tender feelings for at least one of them. This was the adventuress Irene Adler, who appears in the very first short story, "A Scandal in Bohemia". It has been plausibly suggested that the actress Lola Montes, who became the mistress of the King of Bavaria, was the model for Irene, who is the mistress of the King of Bohemia. There were other ways in which Holmes seemed strange and remote to those early readers. He "loathed every form of society with his whole Bohemian soul", injected himself with cocaine, had long periods of total listlessness and depression in which he lay on the sofa scraping at his violin, and was contemptuous of any kind of knowledge that seemed unnecessary to his detective work. The portrait is softened and changed in later stories, when Conan Doyle felt the need to make Holmes's range of knowledge wider and his personality more sympathetic, but he remains essentially superhuman. As Watson says, he was "a man whose knowledge was not that of other mortals".

The choice of Watson as narrator, and as foil to Holmes's acute intelligence, was masterly. For those early readers the doctor was reassuringly like themselves, honest, likeable and determined, conventional enough to be surprised and a little shocked by new ideas, yet always ready for adventure, and prepared to do what seemed to him extraordinary and even ridiculous things in obedience to the commands of his genius friend. He is even prepared to disregard the law at times in deference to the superior justice dispensed by Holmes. The most notable instance is in "Charles Augustus Milverton", where Holmes and Watson see a woman empty "barrel after barrel" of her revolver into the body of an unarmed man. Is this murder? Presumably, but Milverton was a blackmailer, the woman is Lady Eva Bracknell who is about to be married to the Earl of Dovercourt, and the watchers decide to do nothing. As Holmes says to Watson, "we have shared the same room for some years, and it would be amusing if we ended by sharing the same cell." Holmes and Watson are truly complementary figures. One could hardly exist without the other, and they set a pattern of the genius joined to the commonplace which was followed by other detective story writers for more than half a century. Poirot had his Captain Hastings, Doctor Thorndyke his assistant Jervis, Lord Peter Wimsey his valet Bunter, Nero Wolfe his legman Archie Goodwin, Ellery Queen his father the Inspector—in one form or another the Holmes-Watson relationship persisted, although not all detectives were such conspicuous supermen as Holmes nor all assistants as woolly-minded as Watson.

The Holmes stories owed their immense success also to Doyle's talents as a storyteller. It has often been said that as detective puzzles they are limited in scope, that some of them are not very puzzling, and that they are spotted by frequent errors of fact. Conan Doyle said himself that in "Silver Blaze" a story about flat racing, his ignorance cried aloud to

Sherlock Holmes's reputation quickly spread beyond his books. The famous cat artist Louis Wain produced this postcard caricature of actor William Gillette as Holmes around 1900. The handwritten comment at the bottom is from the sender.

Raphael Tuck & Sons' "Louis Wain" Post Card. No. 3885.

WILLIAM GILLETTE AS SHERLOCK HOLMES.

I think this drawing is very clever, notice the revolver.

Louis Wain,

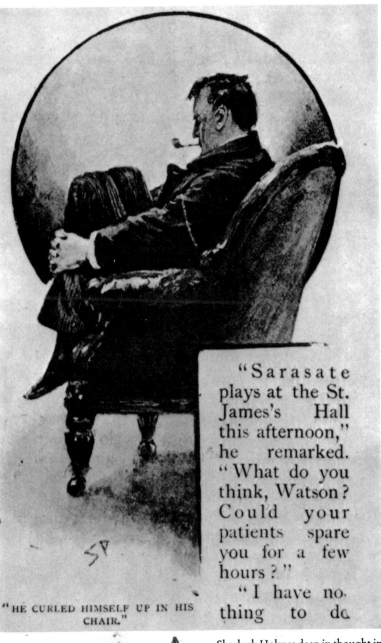

"**S a r a s a t e**
plays at the St.
James's Hall
this afternoon,"
he remarked.
"What do you
think, Watson?
Could your
patients spare
you for a few
hours?"

"I have no-
thing to do

"HE CURLED HIMSELF UP IN HIS
CHAIR."

Sherlock Holmes deep in thought in
'The Red-Headed League'. Sidney
Paget's illustration for *Strand
Magazine*.

Dr Watson (in carriage) in *The Hound of the Baskervilles*. (*below*) The model for Dr Watson: Conan Doyle's secretary Major Wood, shown here (standing) with the author (*circa 1925*).

heaven. Some of his mistakes will be evident to many readers, although one can't agree with the critic of this story who said that if the characters had behaved like this in life, half of them would have been in jail and the other half warned off the turf. But the real point is that the story triumphs over these defects. It is not only that Holmes is at the top of his form, so that the deductions he makes from given facts are as baffling to us as they are to Watson, but that their sparkling lucidity is evident when they have been explained. The story of the horse's disappearance and the mysterious death of his trainer catches our interest immediately, and there are such neat turns in the thirty-odd pages that we are gripped to the end. And "Silver Blaze" is typical of many other stories. One can't say that the flaws in some of them don't matter, but like the inconsistencies in the depiction of Holmes, they are of little importance. What matters is that the twenty best of the sixty short stories can be read again and again with pleasure for particular details (like the poker-bending feat of Dr Grimesby Roylott in "The Speckled Band" which is succeeded by Holmes bending the poker back), for particularly felicitous turns of phrase and neat pieces of characterization, and for the zest with which the tales are told. Of those who wrote crime short stories in Conan Doyle's lifetime only G. K. Chesterton came within measurable distance of him, and this is because Chesterton, like Doyle, was primarily concerned not with planning a puzzle but with telling a tale.

All this still does not quite explain the fascination the stories continue to exert today—does not explain, for example, why my own children should have read through the whole collection of short stories and novels when introduced to them at about the age of ten. Each new generation succumbs, and this is because for every generation they offer something a little different. For those who first read the tales in the *Strand*, the life represented was very much what they saw around them. They knew the distinction between the hansom in "A Case of Identity" which took Miss Sutherland and her mother to the church for her wedding, and the four-wheeler into which Mr Hosmer Angel stepped, and from which he vanished. They lived in a world where gas lighting was common, the electric lamp and the telephone exciting innovations, and the motor car almost unknown. Most of the stories are set in gas-lit crowded London, but the idea that the country just outside the city (what we would call

A Victorian police lamp, often used to shed light on the Sherlock Holmes mysteries.

the Home Counties) was potentially even more sinister thrilled Conan Doyle's mostly urban readers. In the city, Holmes says to Watson, the machinery of justice is always near at hand. "But look at these lonely houses, each in its own fields . . . Think of the deeds of hellish cruelty, the hidden wickedness which may go on, year in, year out, in such places, and none the wiser."

It was a world also in which class distinctions were generally accepted as facts of life, so that it was natural for aristocrats with names like Holdhurst or St Simon or Prendergast to obtain respect from the lower orders (never called the working class, and represented by grocers, housekeepers, commissionaires and poultry sellers), and also from the middle class, the country squires, and the aspiring young Cockneys who frequently appear in the stories. The Duke of Holdernesse, who in "The Priory School" deliberately arranges the kidnapping of his innocent younger son for the sake of his guilty step-brother, gets off much more easily than if he had been a city clerk or a grocer.

For us the stories are very different. What attracts us is their period charm. How amusing that a detective should go down by train to investigate a case, and then take a fly up from the station. How pleasantly out of date is the world in which deference is paid by one class to another, how slowly everything goes on, how quaint are the clothes, manners and speech of these people. The distinction is that for Victorian and Edwardian readers Holmes's world was, more or less, the one they knew; for a later generation like my own—I still just remember a few horse-drawn cabs—it was the day before yesterday; and for succeeding generations it is and will be a society in some ways as remote as that of powdered wigs and doublets, yet in its motives and its actions in many respects little removed from our own.

In the end Conan Doyle became reconciled to Sherlock Holmes who had been, he admitted, "a good friend to me in many ways", but he always found it hard to accept the idea that he might be remembered primarily as the author of these stories. When, a year or two before he died, he was lecturing in Amsterdam and his hosts asked him to say a few words about Sherlock Holmes, he refused with less than his usual courtesy. Yet these stories reflected his character more closely than most of his other writings, for whatever may have been Holmes's conscious origins in Dr Bell, he had his roots in the character of Arthur Conan Doyle. In the course of Conan Doyle's life there are passages that reflect the romantic and incisive Sherlock Holmes, while at other times his conduct and attitudes seem the mirror image in which we see the sober-sided middle class respectable figure of Dr Watson.

"I CLAPPED A PISTOL TO HIS HEAD."

Sidney Paget illustrations for two Sherlock Holmes
stories: 'The Beryl Coronet' (*above*) and 'The Brazilian
Cat'. (*r.*) Both first appeared in *Strand Magazine*.

"I HURLED MYSELF THROUGH THE GAP."

The Doyle coat of arms.

Conan Doyle (age 6) with his
father, Charles Doyle.

Grandfather John Doyle—the
political cartoonist 'HB'.

CHAPTER TWO
THE YOUNG MAN

Arthur Conan Doyle was born in Edinburgh on May 22, 1859. He was the second child and eldest son of Charles Doyle, who worked as assistant to the surveyor in the Scottish Office of Works. In many cases the family background and early life of famous men can be dismissed in a line or two, but the emotional inheritance that Arthur Conan Doyle received from his family was important to him throughout his life.

The Doyles traced their origins back to France, and to the name of D'Oel or D'Oil, but a branch of the family was established in Ireland by the fourteenth century, and the Doyle coat of arms was ratified in Ireland early in the seventeenth century. The Doyles were ardent Catholics, and suffered for it by being dispossessed of their lands. They were a considerable clan, who emerge into written history with the birth of Arthur's grandfather John Doyle in 1797.

John Doyle studied art in Dublin, left to try his luck in London when he was twenty, and became under the pseudonym HB the most celebrated political cartoonist of the Regency period. He had four sons who

A watercolour by James Doyle for his
History of England.

UP AND DOWN
POLITICAL SEE-SAW

possessed artistic talent, and three of them became well known. James was a painter and scholar who produced an illustrated history of England, Henry began as a painter and eventually became director of the National Gallery of Ireland, and Richard or Dicky Doyle achieved celebrity as one of the most famous artists working for *Punch*. He designed the magazine's cover, showing Mr Punch's long nose and upturned chin, which was used for more than a century. All three were strict Catholics, and Dicky resigned from *Punch* because of its opposition to the Pope's plan to create a Catholic archbishopric and a dozen bishoprics in England.

Charles was the youngest of the brothers. Like the rest of them he possessed artistic talent, but unlike the others was unable to turn it to commercial use. He got the post in the Scottish Office of Works in 1849, when he was only seventeen, but never improved his position, and his salary which on his appointment was £180 a year never rose above £250. He supplemented this by doing some book illustration, and selling a few of his paintings, but these were probably too fantastic to be popular, and he gave away as many as he sold. The early biographies of Conan Doyle depicted his father as a dreamy aesthetic figure "with exquisite manners and an unbrushed top hat", who was never unkind to his children, but in a casual way neglected them. More recently it has become known that Charles Doyle was an epileptic and an alcoholic. He left his job at the

Office of Works while in his late forties, and most of the years between this time and his death in 1893 were spent in nursing homes for alcoholics, and mental homes. The illustrated diary he kept in one of these homes shows the fantastic nature of his talent, and also his interest in fairies. Girl fairies emerge from flowerpots or are embedded in holly, there are enormous birds very exactly drawn, fairy music stools and an elf's umbrella appear, drawn with whimsical humour. The diary reinforces the view that Charles Doyle was a man quite unable to cope with the problems of everyday life.

All the coping was done by his wife Mary, who was both Irish and Catholic, and who, although her father was nothing more aristocratic than a doctor, traced her descent back on her mother's side to connection with the Plantagenets. The Ma'am, as she was called by her children, had a passionate pride in her lineage, and encouraged Arthur to take an interest in genealogy. She was a well-read woman and a great story-teller, and Arthur afterwards said that he owed his first interest in literature to her skill as a teller of tales, and her art of "sinking her voice to a horror-stricken whisper when she came to a crisis in her narrative". Mary must also have been a good manager. There were ten children, of whom five girls and two boys survived, and they "lived in the hardy and bracing atmosphere of poverty", as Arthur later said. It was unthinkable that a Doyle should not go to one of the two great Catholic boarding schools, Downside and

Mary Doyle. 'The Ma'am'.

Stonyhurst, yet there was no money to send Arthur there. The problem was solved when the Jesuits at Stonyhurst agreed to accept Arthur Conan Doyle without payment, in the hope that he might dedicate his life to a career in the church.

These were the elements that made the character of Arthur Conan Doyle. He adored his mother, wrote long and frank letters to her over many years in which he addressed her as "dearest", and remained close to her until her death at the age of eighty-three. He took from her a strong practical sense, a deep pride in family and country, and a determination to succeed in any enterprise in which he engaged. With his father he had no sense of fellowship, and as a child must surely have resented his father's aloofness and idleness, and perhaps seen his alcoholism. Yet that streak of otherworldliness in Charles Doyle was inherited by the boy, and so was the feeling for fantasy that produced Charles' weirdly fanciful drawings. In later years he thought more tenderly of his father, regarding him as by far the greatest artist in the family ("more terrible than Blake"), and in 1924 he organized an exhibition of Charles Doyle's work. The very first drawings showing Sherlock Holmes were made by Charles Doyle for the original edition of *A Study in Scarlet*. They show a Holmes quite remote from the author's conception, a mild round-faced figure resembling the artist himself.

But all of this was far ahead. Arthur spent two years at the preparatory school of Hodder, and then five at Stonyhurst itself. The teaching was rigid, the food Spartan (dry bread and hot well-watered milk for breakfast, a joint once a week), and corporal punishment savage and frequent. The boy endured rather than liked it, but still did very well. He was good at all sports, but excelled at cricket, and at sixteen passed his matriculation examination with honours, rather to his own surprise. He spent a year at a Jesuit school in Austria, and then had to decide on a vocation. It was settled that he should go in for a medical career, less because he had an inclination for it than from the fact that he would be able to save money while a student by living at home. He worked hard in the hope of getting a scholarship, and was told that he had won a bursary of £40 a year, but through a series of official mistakes he did not receive it, and was put off with a mere £7. This was a hard blow, for his eldest sister was already sending money home from a job in Portugal, and two younger girls

(*above*) A typical Charles Doyle fantasy
painting, and (*below*) one of his
illustrations for *A Study in Scarlet*.

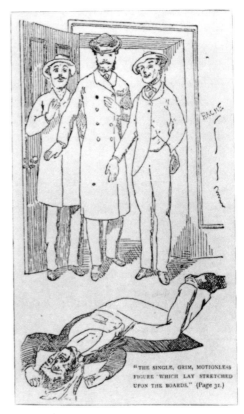

"THE SINGLE, GRIM, MOTIONLESS
FIGURE WHICH LAY STRETCHED
UPON THE BOARDS." (Page 31.)

were about to take up jobs. It was five years before, taking his degree as Bachelor of Medicine at Edinburgh, in 1881, he was able to do the same; five years of what he called a "long weary grind at botany, chemistry, anatomy, physiology, and a whole list of compulsory subjects, many of which have a very indirect bearing upon the art of curing." He was fascinated by Dr Bell, and impressed by the anatomist Professor Rutherford, but otherwise he took away little from Edinburgh except his degree, and the background knowledge that served him so well in the creation of Sherlock Holmes.

His father had retired to a nursing home while Arthur was a student, and the young man must often have felt himself a burden on the family. At the end of his second year he took a summer job with a local doctor, and he was optimistic about his prospects. He wrote to the Ma'am:

> Let me once get my footing in a good hospital and my game is clear. Observe cases minutely, improve in my profession, write to the *Lancet*, supplement my income by literature . . . and then when my chance comes be prompt and decisive in stepping into an honorary surgeonship.

That was how he saw the future, but he felt the duty of making money

THE "EIRA" ARCTIC RELIEF EXPEDITION UNDER CAPTAIN SIR ALLEN YOUNG — THE EXPLORING STEAM VESSEL "HOPE"

In 1880, Conan Doyle went on a seven-month voyage to the Arctic as a ship's doctor on a whaler. On one occasion he nearly drowned in the icy waters, and he was so enthusiastic in the hunt for whales that the captain offered to make him a harpooner as well as a doctor.

(*l.*) The steam vessel *Hope*, some two
years after Doyle sailed in it.

(*above*) A contemporary impression of
the Arctic.

now. He wrote and sold a short story or two, and then signed on as ship's surgeon, even though he was only a third year student, to a whaler making a seven month visit to the Arctic. He was by now a bulky and almost giantesque figure, a good boxer (he had a successful bout with the steward of the whaler on his first night out) and all-round sportsman, and a man of great physical strength. The trip to the Arctic fulfilled his romantic desire for action and adventure. He was astonished that the Arctic regions were so near. No more than four days out from Shetland they were among drift ice, with a huge seal lying sleek and imperturbable upon one of the swaying white lumps, and the blue sky contrasting with the dazzlingly bright ice that covered the whole sea. He must have enjoyed this voyage as much as any of the journeys he made in later life, and he had the pleasure of being able to give something like fifty pounds to the Ma'am at the end of it. It was in gold pieces, which he concealed in every pocket so that she might have the pleasure of hunting them out. He made a second trip the following year, after taking his B.M., this time as ship's doctor at a salary of £12 a month, on a 4,000 ton steamer taking passengers and cargo to the west coast of Africa. This trip, however, was much less enjoyable. He became extremely ill, presumably with malaria, in Lagos, and spent several days "fighting it out with Death in a very small ring and without a second". He returned with money to give to the Ma'am, and ready now to set up his plate as a doctor.

An impetuousness that often marked his actions led him to a rash move. One of his few friends among the medical students had been a man named Budd, a fine but frenetic Rugby forward with an uncontrollable temper that often led him into trouble, but possessed of a personal magnetism that charmed Conan Doyle. Soon after his return from Africa he received a telegram from Budd at Plymouth, saying that his success there was colossal, and that there was plenty of room for Conan Doyle as partner. In Plymouth he found that Budd had indeed developed a tremendous practice in a few months. He gave consultations free, but patients paid for their medicine so that the result was much the same as if they had been charged for consultations, yet still his waiting rooms, stairs and passages were crammed with people. Conan Doyle was delighted by Budd's unorthodoxy, and by the way in which he shouted at patients and joked with them. Sometimes he addressed them collectively from the

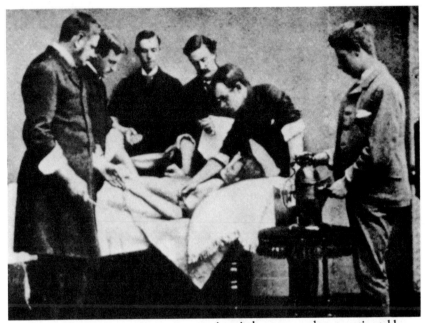

A typical scene around an operating table
when Conan Doyle was a medical student.
The apparatus on the right is a carbolic spray.

landing, at other times made them swear to a course of conduct on an old
volume of medical jurisprudence which he told them was the Bible.

Conan Doyle's plate was put up, he was given a room, and he handled
surgical cases that Budd found uninteresting. He began to build up a
practice, although he was disturbed at times by his friend's methods and
by his lavish use of drugs. He was also astonished by the variety of Budd's
interests, which ranged from the production of advertisements for "Dr
Budd's blood-tonic" to the invention of the Budd Spring-Shutter Screen
for the protection of ships against artillery fire. Budd also had a plan to
emigrate to South America, where he would make a fortune as an eye
specialist. There was a whole continent, he said, without a man in it who
could correct an astigmatism. How could one fail to make money, if one
went round selling thousands of pairs of spectacles, preceded by an agent
who said that the great Signor Budd would be in town next week, ready
to deal with squints, cataracts, or any other eye troubles?

SHERINGHAM,
NORFOLK.

Captain Hay Doyle.
R A.

Rᵧ.

Alum. $\overline{3}p$.

Aᵧ ad $\overline{3}$viii

Sig

The Gargle

To be used 3 times a day.

Arthur Conan Doyle
m D

A rare prescription from Dr Conan
Doyle in 1904—thirteen years after he
had given up medicine as a career.

Conan Doyle listened, and if he did not wholly believe he was certainly fascinated. But the happy relationship did not last long. Conan Doyle's correspondence with the Ma'am has already been mentioned. Budd seemed to her no more than a shady adventurer, and she did not hesitate to say so. When Budd, or his wife, found some of these letters, Budd acted against his friend in a way that revealed the malice behind his extravagant high spirits. Budd's manner changed, and "more than once I caught his fierce grey eyes looking furtively at me with a strange sullen expression." Then Budd said that he was damaging the practice and Conan Doyle, whose own temper was always on a short fuse, said that was easily put right, and wrenched his nameplate from the door. It was agreed that he should start elsewhere and he picked on Portsmouth, choosing it because he knew Plymouth, and thought that Portsmouth seemed a similar town. Budd, with whom his relations now seemed friendly again, said that he would allow Conan Doyle a pound a week until he got on his feet in the new practice.

After a few days Conan Doyle found a house named Bush Villa in Southsea, and put up his plate. He rented the house, giving as references his uncle Henry and Budd. Within a few days he received a letter from Budd, which said that a letter from his mother had been found torn up in his room. When pieced together, it was found to contain references to Budd as "unscrupulous" and "a bankrupt swindler". The Budds must therefore refuse to have anything more to do with him, and of course were cutting off the pound a week.

The story was a lie, for Conan Doyle found the letter in a pocket. He realized that the Budds had been reading his correspondence, and that his financial ruin had been planned, for without the pound a week he was almost penniless. The Ma'am saved him by making up the money from her own small savings, no doubt with a lecture on his unwise choice of friends. It is interesting that in spite of all this Conan Doyle could never bring himself to dislike Budd, who died a few years later, with his practice in decline. He had become convinced that somebody was trying to poison him, and tested each dish at every meal with a complicated chemical apparatus. Conan Doyle called him half-genius, half-quack, put a lively portrait of him into an early autobiographical novel *The Stark Munro Letters*, and used him as a model for some of the erratic, unbalanced but gifted characters who appear in the stories.

He practised in Southsea for eight years. He made £164 in the first year, £250 in the second, and in the whole time never passed £300. He added to this a small income, at first no more than a few pounds a year, from writing short stories. Then he thought that it was necessary to have your name on the back of a volume if you wanted to become known, and wrote *The Firm of Girdlestone*, which is perhaps no worse than most first novels although it was rejected by several publishers and did not reach print for some years. Undeterred, he wrote *A Study in Scarlet*, and as we have seen sold it for £25. But his ambition lay in the field of the historical novel, and he worked industriously at the research and then the writing of a book he called *Micah Clarke*. It was set against the background of Monmouth's rebellion, and it shows Conan Doyle's sympathy for the austerity and integrity of the Puritans, as well as his attempt to emulate the ease and dramatic sense of Macaulay as historian. The book appeared

A mediaeval battle scene from a 14th-century Froissart manuscript. *The White Company* and *Sir Nigel* are both set in the Middle Ages.

Louise Hawkins, Conan Doyle's first
wife, who died in 1906.

Bush Villa
Southsea
March 14th /90

Dear Hemsyley

Many thanks for your note. I
have forwarded a copy of "The Sign of Four"
for Mr Palmer. Lippincott is so little read as
yet that the story is fresh to the public. Yet I
should never have thought of ~~the~~ using it as
a serial had I not had several unsolicited
requests from different papers. So I thought
I might as well extend it. No other offer in the
Birmingham district. I think the intermediate
syndicate may very well be dispensed with
in transactions between author and editor.

Saw Longmans yesterday. The Polestar
was sold right out in a day. They are now
reprinting, and no doubt your copy will
reach you then. "Mysteries & Adventures" is a
pirated edition of tales written years ago in
London Society — some of them when I was
little more than a boy. It is rough on me
having these youthful effusions brought out
in this catchpenny fashion, but I have no
legal redress. The less reviewed or read they are
the better. So glad you liked Micah. He has

Letter written by Conan Doyle in 1890,
referring to several of his books.
Lippincott was the American publisher
of *The Sign of Four*.

made some warm friends. I am on a historical novel now "The White Company" which I think will be better than Micah.

With kindest regards
Yours very truly
A Conan Doyle.

in 1889 and was an immediate success, with four editions being called for in a few months. In these years at Southsea he continued to write short stories, produced the second Sherlock Holmes novel *The Sign of the Four*, and wrote another historical novel, *The White Company*, which he considered one of his finest works. "That's done it," he cried as he wrote the last words, and hurled his inky pen across the room. He was right, in the sense at least that *The White Company* was even more successful than *Micah Clarke*.

Yet it would be wrong to suggest that at Southsea he devoted himself to writing books rather than to medicine. During these years he looked to the money that came from fiction as an addition to his income, not as his mainstay. The first years were not easy. His ten year old brother Innes came to live with him. Conan Doyle sent him to a local day school, tried to act as a father to the boy, and incidentally helped to ease the financial pressure on the Ma'am in Edinburgh. They did not have much to live on at Southsea. Innes wrote to the Ma'am: "The patients are crowding in. We have made three bob this week. We have vaxenated a baby and got hold of a man with consumtion [sic]."

For a while the brothers lived alone, then they let the ground floor to a woman who kept house for them. In 1885 Conan Doyle married Louise Hawkins, the elder sister of a young patient who died. The sweet and docile Louise was from the first a rather shadowy figure. Conan Doyle was a good husband and, when his first child Mary was born in 1889 a good father, but one part of him was essentially a man of action. He lived his life as a doctor, enjoyed playing for Portsmouth both at cricket and soccer, and played his part in the life of the town.

All this, however, was not enough. In 1890 a German doctor announced that he had discovered a cure for consumption which he would demonstrate in Berlin, and Conan Doyle decided that he must go and see it. He had not specialized in consumption, so that the impulse is not easily explained. It is tempting to believe that it sprang from the super-rational element in his nature, and that it showed an advance knowledge of the fact that in three years' time Louise would be found to have consumption

The title page from the 1893 edition of *Micah Clarke.*

and would be given only a few months to live. Whether or not this was so, he went to Berlin. The trip was useless, because he could not get into the demonstration, but on the journey home he talked to a Harley Street skin specialist who said that he ought to leave the provinces and general practice, and set up as a specialist in London. What kind of specialist? Well, Doyle was interested in work on the eye (had he been influenced by Budd's scheme to make a fortune by prescribing spectacles in South America?), and the Harley Street man suggested that he should do six months' work in Vienna and then start up in London. No sooner said than done. The Southsea practice was abandoned (it was too small to be sold), Mary sent to her grandmother, and Conan Doyle and the acquiescent Louise set off for Vienna.

This hare-brained scheme was obviously destined for failure, and fail it did. The lectures were in German, and although Conan Doyle had a fair conversational knowledge of the language he could not follow the technical terms, and soon gave up attending them. He wrote a short book called *The Doings of Raffles Haw*, and left Vienna after two months instead of six. When the couple returned he set up in practice in Devonshire Place, at the top of Wimpole Street. It was a splendid location, quiet and ideal for writing. Not a single patient crossed the threshold, and he sat in his consulting room from ten in the morning until four in the afternoon writing stories, the early Sherlock Holmes short stories among them. Their immediate success, the lack of patients, and a severe attack of influenza that put his life in danger for a week, decided him. He would trust to writing and make a living from that.

> I remember in my delight taking the handkerchief which lay upon the coverlet in my enfeebled hand, and tossing it up to the ceiling in my exultation. I should at last be my own master. No longer would I have to conform to professional dress or try to please any one else. I would be free to live how I liked and where I liked. It was one of the great moments of exultation in my life.

W. G. Grace clean bowling Conan Doyle. An illustration
from *Memories and Adventures*. On another occasion it was
Doyle who bowled Grace.

CHAPTER THREE
A PUBLIC MAN

Conan Doyle was in his early thirties when he made the decisive break with medicine, and the next ten years showed the full flowering of his character. He emerged during this last decade of the nineteenth century as one of the most influential figures of his generation. To one part of the Victorian public he was famous as the creator of Sherlock Holmes; to another he was the author of historical novels and stories of adventure; but many who were not interested in history or in tales of detection came to appreciate him as a man with a total faith in the Imperial ideal, a writer who was ready and even eager to play a part in public affairs.

His very appearance was a reassurance to those who had been shocked by what they felt to be the immorality of Oscar Wilde's writing and the eroticism of Aubrey Beardsley's drawings into a feeling that modern art and artists were degenerate, a feeling confirmed by Wilde's conviction in 1895 for homosexual activities. Conan Doyle stood over six feet, weighed more than seventeen stone, and looked like a sportsman rather than a man of letters. And he was in fact a games player of much more than average ability. His great game was cricket, at which he was almost up to

Oscar Wilde, whose image as a writer and public figure was so different to Conan Doyle's.

county standard. He played for the MCC against several counties, hit a century in his first match at Lord's , and was as he says a steady and reliable bowler who once dismissed W. G. Grace. He twice took all ten wickets in an innings, and when he was forty-five years old took seven for fifty-one against Cambridgeshire at Lord's. He played soccer also into his forties, was what he calls a fair average amateur boxer, and at billiards was good enough to make breaks of eighty and ninety. It is typical of his modesty that he should say of these sporting skills: "I have never specialized, and have therefore been a second-rater in all things."

Like other thoughtful men and women of his generation, he was much concerned about the truth of religion. He lost his Catholic faith while still in his teens, and announced this at a family conclave attended by his uncles, when the question of his medical future was being discussed. He refused therefore to proclaim himself as a Catholic doctor. The uncles were deeply shocked, and a rift was created that was never fully healed. For a time he was mildly agnostic, but this stage did not last long. At Southsea he had taken part in experiments which convinced him that telepathic thought transference was possible. He had also investigated Oriental beliefs and religions, and had been attracted by the theosophical creed that the truths found in nature are deeper and more profound than those of empirical science. In 1893, however, he joined the Psychical Research Society, and from that time onwards became more and more interested, at first with a high degree of scepticism, in the spiritualist movement.

His personal life was less happy. He refused to accept the verdict of other doctors that Louise had only a short time to live, and he took her first to Switzerland and then to various places recommended as being helpful to tuberculous patients. He had been told by Grant Allen, a fellow writer and sufferer from the disease, that Allen had benefited greatly by living at Hindhead in Surrey, and there Conan Doyle built a large comfortable house—what he called a considerable mansion. A private power plant provided what in the country was still the new-fangled electric light. The house, Undershaw, was Louise's home until she died in 1906.

The strain of caring so tenderly for his sick wife showed in a certain briskness and curtness with his children—a son, Kingsley, had been born in 1892. To them he was a loved but slightly fearsome figure, although at times he would behave with a boyish irresponsibility that became less

Love from us both.

J.C.D.

A C D

Conan Doyle made several visits to Eygpt. He is shown here at the Pyramids with his second wife, Jean. On another print of the photo, he wrote: "Everyone happy except the donkey."

frequent with the years. Part of the strain came no doubt from his meeting in 1897 with a young woman named Jean Leckie. If one needed evidence that Conan Doyle was not merely a typical but a super-typical man of the period, it would be provided by the fact that his relations with Jean Leckie, who was fourteen years his junior, remained platonic until after Louise had died. After that they married, and she bore him three children. He told the Ma'am of his attachment, and she understood and approved his conduct. He also told his brother-in-law Willie Hornung, author of the Raffles stories, and was angry when both Hornung and his wife Connie were critical of Conan Doyle. Hornung said that he could not see it mattered whether or not the affair was platonic, and Conan Doyle responded that it made all the difference between guilt and innocence. Hornung's tone, Conan Doyle told the Ma'am, "was that of an attorney dissecting a case, instead of a brother standing by a brother in need". The quarrel was mended but, as he said, the strain of living for years in a sick room was great.

Conan Doyle with Kingsley, the son from his first marriage (*circa* 1900).

The marriage of Conan Doyle and Jean Leckie took place
at St. Margaret's, Westminster, on 18th September, 1907.
The best man was C. D.'s brother, Innes (r.).

He escaped into his study, and escaped also into public life. He attended
dinners, joined literary clubs and societies, went on trips with friends,
wrote a curtain raiser called *Waterloo*, which was put on at the Lyceum
with the great Henry Irving in the main part, and then a sporting comedy
called *The House of Temperley* which was also staged with success. He took
his young brother Innes, who was about to become an Army subaltern,
to the United States, where he carried out a tour in which he gave talks
and readings. The Americans took to him in a big way, liking his bluff
manner, his cheerfulness, his sympathetic voice with its Scots accent.
They appreciated his simplicity and unpretentiousness, the total absence
in him of what they thought of as English "side" or swank. And Conan
Doyle was delighted both by the people and the country, by the great
spaces between cities and the openness and vigour of a people whom he
felt to be very much his own kind.

Sherlock Holmes in *The Valley of Fear*.
Illustration by Frank Wiles for *Strand
Magazine*.

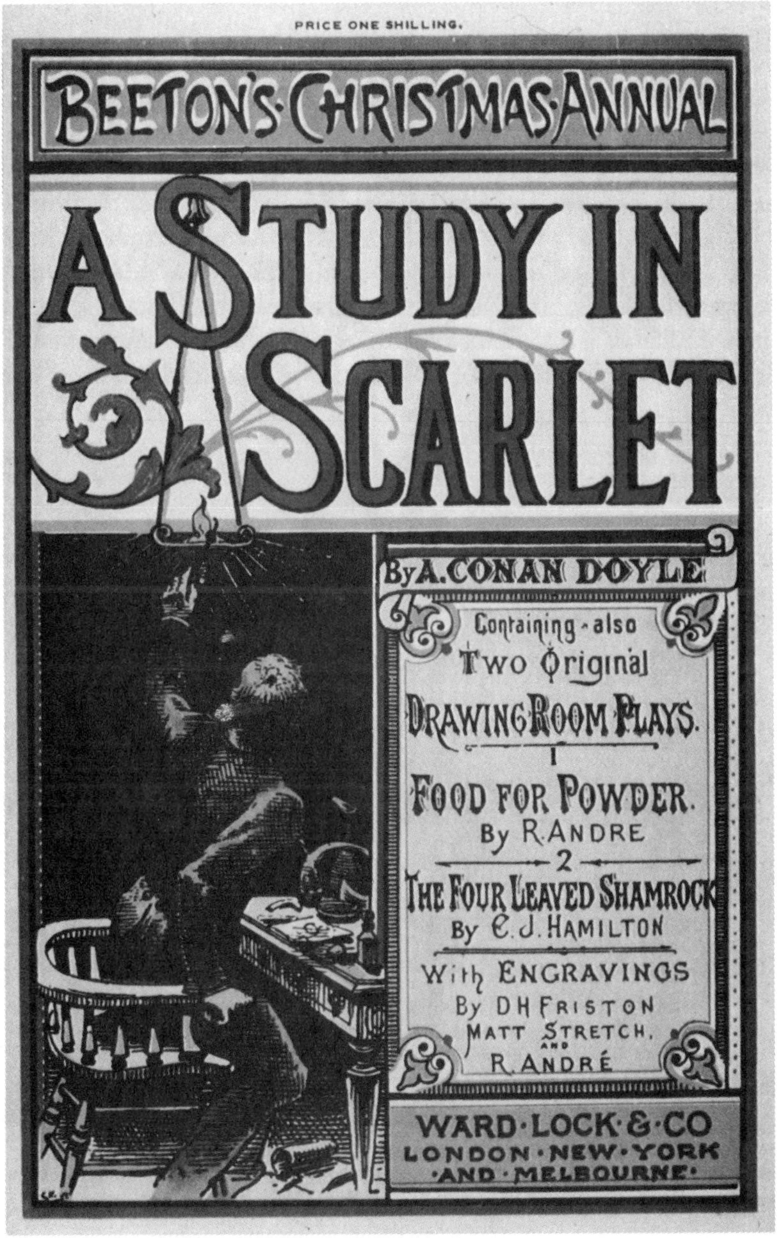

PRICE ONE SHILLING.

BEETON'S CHRISTMAS ANNUAL

A STUDY IN SCARLET

By A. CONAN DOYLE

Containing also
Two Original
DRAWING ROOM PLAYS.
1
FOOD FOR POWDER.
By R. ANDRE
2
THE FOUR LEAVED SHAMROCK
By C. J. HAMILTON

With ENGRAVINGS
By D H FRISTON
MATT STRETCH,
AND
R. ANDRÉ

WARD·LOCK·&·CO
LONDON·NEW·YORK
AND·MELBOURNE·

The first appearance of Sherlock Holmes: *A Study in Scarlet*, published in *Beeton's Christmas Annual* in 1887. Conan Doyle was paid the grand fee of £25.

The Americans thought themselves prosaic, but he told them that the history of the redskin and the trapper was just as romantic as that of knights and archers, castles and abbeys. Behind the sound of cable cars and telephone bells he heard the woodman's axe and the scout's rifle. He left strong in the certainty of the grandeur of America's future, and of the special bond that existed between America and Britain. "We've got to go into partnership with them or be overshadowed by them," he wrote to a friend. This was a theme to which he often returned, as in a speech made in 1912 when he said that when he looked at the flag of St George and the flag of George Washington, "it is so obvious that the future of the world lies in our hands". The Americans loved the Holmes stories as much as the British, and for many years Conan Doyle was probably the best-known and most popular Englishman in the United States.

On tour in America. (*l.*) Conan Doyle's lecture notes.

(*above*) With a shooting companion.

He emerged as a public figure during the Boer War, which began in October 1899. Before Christmas, in what was known as Black Week, the British suffered three staggering defeats at the hands of this nation of farmers who fought on horseback, hit their enemy hard and then slipped away, and as one of the British Generals complained, simply did not fight according to the accepted rules. There was much alarm in Britain, together with an upsurge of national feeling, and on Christmas Eve Conan Doyle decided to volunteer for South Africa. The Ma'am was both angry and distressed. Wasn't his life of more value to his country at home? There were hundreds of thousands who could fight, she said, but only one who could have created Sherlock Holmes. And then surely his sympathies, like hers, would be with the hard-working Boers rather than with greedy money-grubbers like "Rhodes and Co". What he felt, she said, was an impulse from the old fighting blood of his ancestors, the Plantagenet Percys and the Irish Doyles and Conans. It was a mere fever, and he must resist it.

Her feelings about the Boers were shared by many. The discovery of gold in the Witwaterstrand in the 1880s had led many thousands who wanted to get rich quick to go to Johannesburg, which was colloquially known as Jewburg. Cecil Rhodes had strong feelings for the Imperial ideal, but this fitted in very well with his various commercial enterprises. Conan Doyle himself admired and respected the Boers, but his adherence to Britain and the Empire was unquestioning. He answered his mother by saying that she must not blame him, because he had learned patriotism from her. He went on:

> What I feel is that I have perhaps the strongest influence over young men, especially young athletic sporting men, of any one in England . . . It is really important that I should give them a lead. It is not merely my 40 year-old self— though I am as fit as ever I was, but it is the influence I have over these youngsters.

He may have exaggerated the extent of his influence. "It is impossible to be near the great historical events and not to desire to take part in them, or at least to observe them," he had written a few years earlier, and this instinct to move towards excitement was what moved him most, as it did often during his life. The Army showed little interest in the 40 year old volunteer, simply putting him on a waiting list, and when the chance came to join a hospital unit which a friend named John Langman was sending out to South Africa at his own expense, he agreed immediately. His post was that of doctor and unofficial supervisor. In the weeks before they left he evolved a scheme for turning a rifle into "a sort of portable howitzer" by firing it up into the air so that the bullet would drop vertically. The War Office declined to take an interest in it.

One of the first things he did on arriving in Cape Town was to visit the Boer prisoners behind barbed wire at the local racecourse, so that he could distribute money he had been given for charitable purposes. He found the general effect they produced "formidable". They were shaggy, dirty and unkempt, but he thought had the bearing of free men. The pattern of the war had changed when Roberts and Kitchener took overall

Mr. Conan Doyle.   Mr. Langman.

THE LANGMAN FIELD HOSPITAL FOR SOUTH AFRICA: THE INSPECTION OF THE STAFF BY THE DUKE OF CAMBRIDGE AT THE
VICTORIA AND ST. GEORGE'S BARRACKS.

The Duke.   What is it? What's that?
A.C.O.   Please, it's only me!

command, with the weight of British arms being used to defeat the Boers when they were unwise enough to engage in pitched battle. Bloemfontein was captured, and then Pretoria.

The volunteer hospital followed Roberts's advance, and was fully occupied. There was an outbreak of enteric fever, and the hospital equipped for fifty patients was burdened with a hundred and twenty. It was sited on a cricket field, with the pavilion as chief ward, and the floor between the beds was littered with sick or dying men. A haze of flies hung over everything. Twelve of the staff contracted the disease, and three died of it. The Langman Hospital was no worse than others, and sixty men a day were lowered into shallow graves, wrapped in brown blankets. The month during which the epidemic raged was the severest medical test of Dr Conan Doyle's life. At last, however, the local waterworks was captured, conditions improved, and for a few days he was let free to join the Army and see some active soldiering for the first time. He reacted with the enthusiasm that was one of the most attractive aspects of his nature. He admired the speed with which the railway engineers

A press cutting of the Langman Field Hospital on parade,
a few days before their departure for South Africa in
February, 1900. With additional comments from C.D.

A photograph taken at the turn of the
century. Conan Doyle's uniform is
strangely nondescript.

mended damaged lines, the endurance and cheerfulness of the men and the coolness of gunners under fire. He talked politics with captured Boers, and got the impression that they were tired of the war. He gave first aid to a New Zealander wounded in arm and stomach, but hesitated to take out the Mauser bullet with his pen knife, because "that had better be left for chloroform and the field hospital". When he mentioned his name, the man said: "I've read your books." In a private memorandum Conan Doyle congratulated himself on feeling little nervousness, although "I could not have been as perfectly motionless as the Gunners—it was a wonderful exhibition of nerve."

With the capture of the Boer capital Pretoria, the war seemed to be over, and Conan Doyle left for home again early in July, after being in South Africa a little more than three months. He had found the time deeply satisfying, taking delight in the physical activity, the great empty world of the veldt seen in the fresh morning light, trains roaring through darkness at night, dark groups silhouetted against the flame of camp fires. "Wonderful is the atmosphere of war," he wrote, and however differently we may feel, it should be possible to understand his exhilaration.

Before leaving he interviewed Roberts, obtained a number of first-hand accounts of the campaign, and on his return wrote *The Great Boer War*. The book was outdated by the massive *Times History* published a few years later, and also by the fact that the war was not over, as he thought when he wrote, but continued as guerrilla warfare for almost another two years. His story of the war is too impressionistic and inaccurate to be regarded as serious military history, but it remains readable, an account marked by his characteristic lucidity and vigour. At the time it was very successful, and a last chapter suggesting necessary military reforms caused a great stir. The suggested reforms included the concealment of guns (at Colenso almost two batteries had been lost because of their commander's foolhardiness in pushing them forward ahead of the infantry, quite without cover), the abandonment of cavalry swords and lances, and the development of a smaller but much more highly-trained army of infantry, backed by a national volunteer militia trained through rifle clubs. All this, which today seems merely sensible, shocked the Army establishment of the time, and they were also disturbed by his suggestion that the Army should be made more democratic. "Let us have done with the tailoring,

Sons of the second marriage:
Denis and Adrian Doyle.

Denis (18 months old) with his father.

the too-luxurious habits of the mess, the unnecessary extravagance which makes it so hard for a poor man to accept a commission." This last chapter appeared as a separate article, but although it was much discussed very little was done.

The guerrilla war fought by the Boers for eighteen months brought a severe response on the British side. The Boers fed off the land, moved around constantly, struck at British forces and then vanished. Kitchener, who was in command after Roberts's return to Britain, built a network of blockhouses in an attempt to contain the Boers, continued the policy of burning farms that had been begun by his predecessor, and established concentration camps for Boer women and children burned out or expelled from their farms on the ground that they had helped the enemy. Many of the camps were badly sited and badly run, and few of the women knew anything of elementary health precautions. Epidemics of typhoid and measles swept the camps, the death roll was heavy, and there was a storm of protest in Britain. Pamphlets like "Methods of Barbarism", by the liberal journalist W. T. Stead, were widely read, and the revelations of camp conditions made by Emily Hobhouse shocked many consciences. Conan Doyle wrote a reply putting the British case, called *The War in South Africa: Its Causes and Conduct*. This pamphlet, as he called it, was

roughly three times the length of the book you are reading, and it was put together (much of it was quotation from eye witnesses) in little more than a week. He made a good case against the accusations that British soldiers had raped Boer women or used dum-dum bullets which expanded on impact, and about the camps said truly enough that for all their shortcomings they were better than the alternative of starvation. The pamphlet had its effect, especially in other European countries, in countering anti-British feeling. It was a propaganda exercise, but one carried out in support of a cause in which the author truly believed.

Before the pamphlet appeared, he had stood for Parliament in the 1900 General Election. He was a Unionist (that is, Conservative) candidate, not in opposition to the Liberal policy of social reform at home, but because the Unionists were supremely the pro-War and Empire party. He stood in central Edinburgh, and was given little chance of winning the strongly Liberal seat, but his storming campaign was immensely effective. His first speech was to workmen in a type foundry, and he gave several impromptu addresses in a day ("I speak in the streets and the people are wonderfully good and nice"), with a formal meeting in the evening. The Operetta house was packed, Princes Street was blocked, he made fourteen speeches in three days. He genially acknowledged the hecklers who called him Sherlock Holmes, and then thumped home the importance of military reforms, national defence, the Empire. On polling day, however, a fanatical Protestant placarded the district with posters saying that Conan Doyle was a Jesuit-educated Catholic agent, an untruth particularly galling to a man who had abandoned his Catholic beliefs. The posters were thought to have swayed many voters, and although Conan Doyle improved the Unionist vote by 1500, he still lost the election. He fought again in 1906, the year of the Liberal landslide, and did less well.

Years later he reflected, probably rightly, that Parliament would have been a dead end for him, because he would never have been a good party man. Electioneering, he said, was a vile business, comparable only to mud baths, which were said to have a purifying effect. But those were not his feelings at the time. "It is now or never," he told his journal in 1900, and his disappointment must have been intense, although it was temporary. His interest in party politics was never very great, but he was by nature a fighter, and fighters never like to lose.

By the time he fought the election he was not only a famous author but also a famous man, and he was offered a knighthood. His immediate instinct was to refuse what he contemptuously called the badge of the provincial mayor. Surely, he said to the Ma'am, she did not suggest that he should accept? Big men did not condescend to such things. "Not that *I* am a big man, but something inside me revolts at the thought . . . All my work for the State would seem tainted if I took a so called 'reward'." But the Ma'am did suggest acceptance, and she persisted even when he said that a knighthood was a discredited title. "I tell you it is unthinkable. Let us drop the subject." The Ma'am was not used to being refused, and in the end she had her way. In 1902 he became Sir Arthur. Years later, in one of the last Sherlock Holmes stories, "The Three Garridebs", Watson mentions in passing that Holmes had refused a knighthood, and named the year. It was 1902.

CHAPTER FOUR
THE CRUSADER

The personality of Arthur Conan Doyle should now be clear. He was in many ways a conventional man of his time. He prided himself on being practical, thought that any man worthy of the name would wish to excel at sports and games, had no patience with those who wished to change the pattern of society, never dreamed of questioning the idea that the British Empire was a great force for moral good wherever the map was coloured red, and was interested in every new scientific development. This was the Conan Doyle who was so intent on physical fitness that in his early forties he took a course of physical development with Eugene Sandow, the most famous "strong man" of the time, who lacked patience with journalists and politicians opposed to the South African War, who owned a motor-car as early as 1903, and three years later installed in the grounds of his country home an electrically powered monorail balanced by a gyroscope. But another Conan Doyle existed within his burly frame, a man deeply unsatisfied by the practicalities of this world because of his certainty that there was something beyond them. This second Conan Doyle became more and more interested in spiritualism as the years passed, and it was he who wrote the poem "The Inner Room", about the multiple personalities existing in us all:

> There are others who are sitting
>   Grim as doom,
> In the dim ill-boding shadow
>   Of my room,
> Darkling figures, stern or quaint,
> Now a savage, now a saint,
> Showing fitfully and faint
>   In the gloom.

This Conan Doyle was capable also of actions that transcended the commonsense of a flag-waving patriot, as in the petition he drew up in 1916 for the reprieve of Sir Roger Casement from sentence of execution. Casement had supported the German cause as soon as World War I started, and had landed in Ireland to foment an insurrection against

69

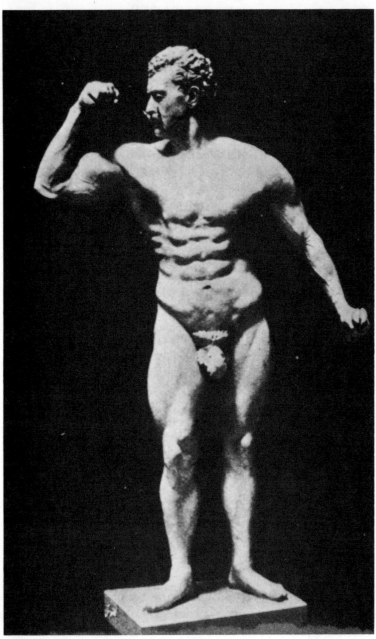

Plaster cast of Eugene Sandow, the most famous 'strong
man' of his time. Conan Doyle when in his forties took a
course of physical development with him.

British rule. By Conan Doyle's code he was a traitor. He was also, as the British Government revealed by allowing the secret circulation of his diaries, a homosexual, and Conan Doyle regarded homosexuality as a pitiable but detestable abnormality. Why then did he support Casement's reprieve, and even contribute liberally to his legal expenses? He no doubt thought about Casement, as he had done about Oscar Wilde, that "the monstrous development which ruined him was pathological" and required hospital treatment; but he said also that "as no possible sexual offence could be as bad as suborning soldiers from their duty", he was not much concerned by it. Conan Doyle had admired Casement's attempt a few years earlier to reveal the barbaric cruelties practised on natives in the Belgian Congo, and regarded his pro-German activities as proof that he was mentally unbalanced. He did not expect the campaign for a reprieve to succeed, but until Casement's execution he carried it through with characteristically single-minded energy. Once he had taken up a cause his

Sir Roger Casement who exposed the atrocities in the Belgian Congo, and was later tried for treason.

~~A Straggler~~

"A Story of Waterloo" Tower Cottage.

Winchelsea.

Sussex.

A thousand congratulations upon the success of your ~~perfect~~ little play —

When I first read it, more than a year ago (two years I think) it moved me strangely," & I wrote to you then & there & —— sent the note into the waste-paper basket! —— I've seen most of the rehearsals, & can see in my mind's eye the

Part of a letter written by the actress
Ellen Terry in 1894, congratulating
Conan Doyle on his play 'Waterloo'.

'Undershaw'—the house built by
Conan Doyle in Hindhead to help
restore his first wife's health.

imagination remained for a while at white heat, so that he thought of almost nothing else. He never forgot the words written to him in adolescence by a family friend, Dr Walter: " 'Do' is a far finer word than 'Believe'; and 'Action' a far surer watchword than 'Faith'."

The Casement crusade was fought with the same intensity that he had given to the Boer War booklet and to his first attempt at winning a Parliamentary seat. In the course of his life he was involved as a crusader in two criminal cases which he fought to the end, in one with partial and in the other with total success. The cases are of especial interest because they show that Conan Doyle himself had some of the powers in observation and deduction that he gave to Sherlock Holmes.

The story of George Edalji began in 1903. His father, Shapurji Edalji, was a Parsee turned Christian, who had been for nearly thirty years vicar of a parish in a mining district near Birmingham. Shapurji Edalji had married an Englishwoman and the family, including their three children, were the butts of practical jokes like the insertion of bogus advertisements under their name in the local paper. They also received occasionally threatening anonymous letters.

The Chief Constable of Staffordshire, Captain Anson, believed that these anonymous letters were being written by George Edalji, even though they threatened his own family with death. When the key of the local Grammar School was found on the Edaljis' doorstep, Anson wrote to Shapurji Edalji that he knew George had been responsible, that he would not believe "any protestations of ignorance which your son may make about the key", and hoped to give the culprit "a dose of penal servitude". This happened in 1895, and Anson failed in his objective because no culprit was found; but he was still Chief Constable in 1903, when there was an outbreak of attacks on horses and cattle in the district. The animals had their stomachs ripped open at night with some sharp shallow instrument, and a new spate of anonymous letters sent to the police and to local residents accused George Edalji of being one among a gang of cattle killers. The local police, no doubt influenced by Anson, identified George Edalji as the letter writer, again in spite of the fact that the letters contained accusations against him. He was a man of twenty-seven, who still lived at home although he practised as a solicitor in Birmingham.

George Edalji, whose case of wrongful imprisonment was successfully taken up by Conan Doyle.

The family home was searched. Very little of importance was found, and there was some ground for suspicion that a piece of evidence relating to Edalji's jacket had been planted by the police. With the help of this evidence, and the word of a handwriting expert who had already been discredited in the case of Adolf Beck when he confidently expressed views that proved totally wrong, Edalji was sent to prison for seven years. The inadequacy of the evidence, and its unsatisfactory nature, caused widespread protests. The ten thousand names on a petition to the Home Office included those of several hundred barristers and solicitors. The petition had no immediate effect, but after serving three years of his sentence Edalji was suddenly released. There was no explanation, and his name had not been cleared. He set out his own account of what had happened to him, and Conan Doyle saw it. "As I read, the unmistakable accent of truth forced itself upon my attention, and I realized that I was in the presence of an appalling tragedy, and that I was called upon to do what I could to set it right."

The reaction is typical, and so is the fact that once moved Conan Doyle went into action immediately. He obtained the papers, read accounts of the trial, went to Staffordshire, visited the scene of the crimes, met George Edalji. The deductions that convinced him of the man's innocence are worthy of Sherlock Holmes. The crime for which Edalji had been convicted had been committed on a rainy moonless night, in the middle of a field. He would have had to walk a mile, twice crossing a main railway line protected by a double fence, or else take a longer route which involved crossing ditches and climbing over hedges and banks. In the first of the articles Conan Doyle wrote in the *Daily Telegraph* he said that five minutes in Edalji's company was enough to convince him of the man's almost certain innocence. They met at a hotel:

> I had been delayed, and he was passing the time by reading the paper . . . He held the paper close to his eyes and rather sideways, proving not only a high degree of myopia but marked astigmatism. The idea of such a man scouring fields at night and assaulting cattle while avoiding the watching police was ludicrous to anyone who can imagine what the world looks like to eyes with myopia of eight dioptres.

So those lectures from the Vienna eye specialist were of some use after all. In addition, Conan Doyle said, he understood that Edalji might rouse suspicion because his sight was "so hopelessly bad that no glasses availed in the open air" and without them he had a vacant staring appearance which looked very odd. "There, in a single physical defect, lay the moral certainty of his innocence."

Then he examined the police evidence in detail, and found it wanting. One of the few pieces of genuine evidence they had found was a damp coat, with stains on it which might have been blood. Two good points, Conan Doyle said, but "unfortunately, they are incompatible and mutually destructive". Since the coat was damp, the presumed bloodstains must have been damp also if they referred to the crime, and then "the inspector had only to touch them and then to raise his crimson finger in the air to silence all criticism". And then these stains were each about the size of a threepenny bit, very small. The comment? "The most adept operator who ever lived would not rip up a horse with a razor upon a dark night and have only two threepenny-bit spots of blood to show for it. The idea is beyond argument."

By the time he had done with the rest of the police case it was in shreds. But if Edalji was innocent, who was guilty? Some quiet enquiries in the district, beginning with investigation of the earlier anonymous letters and the theft of the school key, soon unearthed a suspect named Royden Sharp, one of the school's students who had later been apprenticed to a butcher. "The case . . . is very strong," he wrote to the Ma'am, adding in Holmesian style: "I have five separate lines of inquiry on foot by which I hope to make it overwhelming." His belief that Sharp was guilty must have been confirmed when he too began to receive anonymous letters.

But life is not so tidy as a detective story. Captain Anson had powerful friends, and one of the three Commissioners set up to consider the case in the light of the new evidence was his second cousin. The Commissioners decided that Edalji had been wrongly convicted of horse-maiming, and he would be pardoned. But he might still have written the letters, and in any case had "to some extent brought his troubles on himself", and so would be given no compensation for his three years in prison. Conan Doyle called it a blot on the record of English justice. He commented bitterly on the way in which officials stick together:

What confronts you is a determination to admit nothing which inculpates another official, and as to the idea of punishing another official for offences which have caused misery to helpless victims, it never comes within their horizon.

The other criminal case in which Conan Doyle took up his pen to help a man unjustly accused did not call for deductive powers of the same order, but it became nationally famous as an example of injustice put right. It also, like the Edalji case although for a very different reason, left a bitter after-taste for Conan Doyle.

Oscar Slater, unjustly convicted of murder in 1909. Another of Conan Doyle's crusades.

In 1909 a man who used the name of Oscar Slater was tried in Edinburgh on the charge of murdering with a hammer an old woman named Marion Gilchrist. Slater was a German Jew, his means of making a living were dubious, and at the time of his arrest he had landed in New York with his mistress. Because of all this—the case, like that of Edalji, shows the deep British prejudice against foreigners at that time—all sorts of lurid newspaper stories appeared before the trial. The police investigation was disgracefully slack, to say the least—witnesses had Slater's photograph shown to them in advance before identifying him as a man seen near the victim's house—and the conduct of the trial was no better. The Lord Advocate, who prosecuted, made a number of totally unjustified assumptions about Slater's character and activities (he said, for example, that Slater lived on prostitution without calling anything more than hearsay evidence in support), and the judge did almost nothing to stop him. The defence was inadequate, and the summing-up supported most of the outrageous statements made by the Lord Advocate. Slater was found guilty by a majority verdict. He was sentenced to death, but reprieved two days before the date fixed for his execution. His sentence was commuted to hard labour for life.

Conan Doyle's attention was drawn to the affair in 1910 after publication of a book in the Notable British Trials series which said openly that there had been a miscarriage of justice. He had been deeply angered by the conspiracy of silence over Edalji, and did not want to be involved in any similar affair.

> I went into the matter most reluctantly, but when I glanced at the facts, I saw that it was an even worse case than the Edalji one, and that this unhappy man had in all probability no more to do with the murder for which he had been condemned than I had.

So he went into action again. Slater was in many ways an epitome of the kind of man he disliked. He made his living in ways that were doubtfully honest (mostly by gambling and sharp dealing, although probably not by prostitution). He dressed flashily, and was a rootless cosmopolitan with none of the national pride that Conan Doyle valued so greatly. Yet none of this affected Conan Doyle, any more than he had been affected by Casement's homosexuality in working for his reprieve. He took up Slater's cause, and spent much of his dynamic energy on it, simply to put right a case of judicial injustice.

An artist's impression of Sir Roger
Casement pleading 'Not Guilty' at his
treason trial in 1916.

His first step was to publish an eighty page booklet, *The Case of Oscar Slater*. In this he pointed out the holes in the prosecution evidence, which were so plain that commonsense rather than deductive brilliance was needed to see them, and attacked the prejudice shown by judge and prosecuting counsel. The pamphlet sold widely because of his name, but its reception was lukewarm at best, and in many newspapers distinctly hostile. Conan Doyle was unmoved. His activities, and the statement of a courageous police inspector who said that some of the evidence at the trial bore no relation to the statements originally taken from witnesses, pushed the authorities into ordering an inquiry. This took place in 1914. It was held in secret, and presided over by a Scottish lawyer who had no experience in criminal matters. The witnesses who gave evidence were not on oath. The resulting White Paper completely supported the authorities. A retrial was refused, and the police inspector was dismissed from the force without a pension.

Slater remained in prison. In 1925 he smuggled out a message appealing for help, and on receipt of it Conan Doyle put in train a request for the granting of an official pardon. This was refused, but in 1927 the chief prosecution witness revealed, from the safety of America, that she had originally given the name of another man to the police as that of a person who had often visited Marion Gilchrist, and knew her well. For unknown reasons the police had ignored this information, and according to the witness had practically dictated her final statement. Another witness went back on her evidence, and Slater was released after having, as the Scottish Secretary said, completed more than eighteen and a half years of his life sentence. There was no suggestion that he was innocent, and no mention of compensation.

Conan Doyle immediately wrote a pamphlet which he sent to all M.P.s, saying that a new trial was necessary, and asking them to insist that one should be ordered. At last, after questions in the House of Commons, an appeal was put in hand. It cost money, and Slater had almost nothing, so Conan Doyle guaranteed most of the expenses. The evidence of Slater's innocence presented at the appeal was, or should have been, overwhelming, but as Conan Doyle had found in the Edalji case, "what confronts you is the determination to admit nothing which inculpates another official". The appeal judges decided that the jury's verdict was reasonable, and that the new evidence was not material, but still they found for Slater on the ground that the judge's instructions "amounted to a misdirection in law". So the verdict was put aside, and Slater was found officially not guilty. Conan Doyle wrote: "My own connection with the case ends now that I have succeeded in establishing Slater's innocence."

And the bitter after-taste? Slater, who on his discharge from prison had written a letter of gratitude that began: "Sir Conan Doyle, you breaker of my shackels [sic], you lover of truth for justice sake, I thank you from the bottom of my heart", quarrelled with the man who had been more responsible than any other for securing his release. In part this was because of Conan Doyle's own attitude. He would have nothing to do with Slater personally, and returned the cigar-cutter sent to him by the German as a present. But their quarrel arose over the matter of Slater's compensation, and the repayment of the money spent by Conan Doyle and others in connection with the appeal. Slater was offered the miserable sum of £6000 as compensation for his time in prison, and immediately accepted it. Conan Doyle thought he should have asked for £10,000 plus a claim for legal expenses, but although he regarded the figure as inadequate he thought Slater was bound in honour to repay those who had spent money in connection with the appeal. The amount he was personally out of pocket meant nothing to him, but he felt that Slater had behaved dishonourably. The great Slater case ended with unseemly bickering in newspapers between the victim and the man who had helped to free him. Conan Doyle's feelings were summed up in a letter written to Slater:

If you are indeed quite responsible for your actions, then you are the most ungrateful as well as the most foolish person whom I have ever known.

CHAPTER FIVE
THE AUTHOR

The Sherlock Holmes stories, and to a much less degree the historical novels, made Conan Doyle a famous author, but it was his Boer War activities that gave him the position of a national celebrity, a man likely to be consulted by the authorities on all sorts of matters. During the last decade of the nineteenth century he published eleven novels and five collections of short stories. This furious literary activity slackened as he became occupied with questions ranging from national defence to the Edalji affair, or the crimes of the Belgians in the Congo. He was never again to approach such an output, or to produce work of such quality, and although he continued writing until the year of his death he was in style and feeling altogether a late Victorian.

It seems right therefore to examine his work at this point, before going on to the remainder of his life. Conan Doyle's output as an imaginative writer, distinct from factual histories and pamphlets, falls into three groups: the Sherlock Holmes and other mystery stories, the historical and sporting novels and short stories, and what we would now call the science fiction. There are also a few books that do not fit into any of these categories, and a number of plays. The discussion of them that follows is divided accordingly, but other divisions would be perfectly possible—the short stories, for instance, could be treated as a group on their own. What follows is meant to be helpful rather than definitive.

(i) *The Holmes Books and other mystery stories.* The origins of the Holmes stories, and the basis for our lasting appreciation of them, have already been mentioned. The first three collections of short stories, *The Adventures*, *The Memoirs* and *The Return*, are much superior to the last volumes, *His Last Bow* and *The Case-Book*. The first two belong to the eighteen nineties, and the stories in *The Return* had been completed by 1904. *His Last Bow* appeared in 1917, and *The Case-Book* ten years later. There are good stories in these last volumes, along with some weak ones, but the enthusiastic delight in his own creations that marked the early books is missing. The old master is going through the motions, and doing so with skill, but no longer with pleasure. In part no doubt this comes from the fact that the later stories deal with a time long past. "His Last Bow", which was set in August 1914 just at the beginning of the War, was actually written in 1917, and this was the nearest thing to a con-

A dramatic moment from *The Hound of the Baskervilles*, as it appeared in *Strand Magazine*.

temporary setting in the later stories. The tales written in the nineteen twenties deal with a Victorian or Edwardian England that was by now only a memory to their creator.

Some of the other mystery stories written at intervals over the years make lively reading, and in two cases carry a faint echo of Sherlock Holmes. Both "The Last Special" and "The Man with the Watches" are railway mysteries, the first of them being particularly ingenious, and both contain references to the theories of "an amateur reasoner of some celebrity" in one story, and "a well-known criminal investigator" in the other. These theories get near to the truth of the puzzle in the stories, although they do not uncover it.

The four Sherlock Holmes novels all have their partisans, particularly *The Hound of the Baskervilles* (1902), but not many people would place them on the same level as the short stories. Conan Doyle's genius was expressed in the short detective tale, not the novel. Both *A Study in Scarlet* (1888) and *The Valley of Fear* (1915) give up detection part of the way through, to deal with life in an American Mormon community and

INCEPTION OF MORMONISM—JOSEPH SMITH'S FIRST VISION

Joseph Smith's vision which inspired Mormonism. Part of *A Study in Scarlet* takes place in an American Mormon community.

in a miners' settlement. One reason for this was that Conan Doyle liked writing adventure stories, but he had also run out of detective steam. *The Hound* does not err in this way, but we know the villain's identity two-thirds of the way through the book, something that is displeasing to most modern detective story readers. Conan Doyle lacked the skill in spacing out clues and red herrings throughout a novel which became a commonplace of detective stories in the nineteen twenties. The Sherlock Holmes novels were, from the point of view of plotting, enlarged short stories.

(ii) *The Historical Novels.* It was upon these books, in particular *The White Company* (1891) and *Sir Nigel* (1906) that Conan Doyle placed his chief hopes of being remembered as a writer. He thought, as he said later, that they "would live and would illuminate our national traditions". He was disappointed by critics' reaction to *The White Company* even though it was praised, because they treated it "too much as if it were a mere book of adventure . . . whereas I have striven to draw the exact types of character of the folk then living and have spent much work and pains over it, which seems so far to be quite unappreciated by the critics". *Sir Nigel* seemed to him his high-water mark in literature, and again he was disappointed that the novel received no particular critical recognition.

These books, upon which he spent so many pains, are of all his imaginative writings the least congenial to modern taste. We value his "mere tales of adventure" more highly than he did, because they are so well told. The books he took more seriously, on the other hand, seem to most readers now rhetorical and wooden in much of the writing, and to take an idealistic view of the past that we cannot share. *Micah Clarke* (1889) is an agreeable although conventional historical novel about Monmouth's rebellion, but in *The White Company* Conan Doyle attempted more and achieved less. The picture of fourteenth century life, with its insistence on patriotism and the importance of team spirit seems to be viewing the Middle Ages in Victorian terms, the author's passionate support of the ruling order in society would be disagreeable if it did not seem a little absurd, and most of the characterization is as stiff as the writing. There are fine scenes in the book, like the account of the siege of Villefranche and the discussion of the importance of the English archers in the campaign, but they are produced by the writer of adventure stories. The idea of a

The vainglorious Brigadier Gerard
joins a fox hunt behind the British
lines in 'How the Brigadier Slew the
Fox'.

Knights having swords girded on—from a 14th-century
manuscript. Conan Doyle took great trouble to get the
military details right in his mediaeval novels.

company of knight-errants moved by the mediaeval conception of chivalry even as they fight seems to us today simply to ignore the realities of history. The same criticism applies to the high romanticism of *Sir Nigel*, which shows us characters already met in *The White Company* at an earlier period in their lives. Conan Doyle took great trouble to get right the details about armour and archery, but the people drawing the bow and inside the suit of armour are not human beings as we know them. One of Conan Doyle's sons tells a story of being struck across the face by his father when he casually said that a woman was ugly. "Just remember that no woman is ugly," his father said. Such a chivalric code may be admirable, but it does not equip one to see men and women as they are.

One or two of the less-regarded historical novels are more interesting, partly because their author tried less hard with them. *Uncle Bernac* (1897) has found few admirers, and Conan Doyle himself always felt that there was something wrong with it, but the book has a marvellous opening. Young Louis de Laval, who has escaped to England during the French Revolution, is asked by his Uncle Bernac to return. He does so, ignoring the words "Don't come" written above the letter's seal, and is plunged

The Fall of the Bastille at the onset of the French Revolution, the theme of Conan Doyle's novel *Uncle Bernac*.

One of Sidney Paget's illustrations for
the first edition of *Rodney Stone* in 1896.

The bare-knuckle fighting of the prize ring inspired both *Rodney Stone* and the short story 'The Croxley Master'.

The GREAT FIGHT between MENDOZA and HUMPHRIES, at Stilton, Huntingdonshire, May 6, 1789. (*From an Original Painting.*)

into a series of misadventures which are brilliantly maintained without complete explanation for a full fifty pages. The book falls away, but the portrayal of Uncle Bernac is a good deal more interesting than anything in the two novels Conan Doyle valued so highly. The picture of Napoleon in the final chapter is done in a distinctly starry-eyed manner, alien from the rest of the book. There were times when Conan Doyle tended to identify heroes with dictators.

Most of the other historical novels need little comment because they are inferior versions of those already discussed. *Rodney Stone* (1897), how-ever, is something different. Conan Doyle's love of sport and games shows comparatively seldom in his writing. He wrote very little about

Napoleon reviewing the Imperial Guard. The Napoleonic Wars provided the background for the Brigadier Gerard stories.

cricket or football, almost nothing about billiards, fishing or golf. But he did write a novel and some good short stories about boxing, and both *Rodney Stone* and the long short story "The Croxley Master" display his narrative and descriptive powers at their peak.

Conan Doyle said that he thought nobody but a fighting man could fully appreciate some of the detail in *Rodney Stone*, and the book gives scope to his feelings that the old bare-knuckle fighting of the prize ring was "an excellent thing from a national point of view". Its success depended upon people who like himself loved what he called the chivalry of sport, and he noted that the standards of British boxing had been corrupted during the nineteenth century by "the villainous mobs" who were concerned only with making money by betting. *Rodney Stone* is set in the chivalric time and it views the great fighters of the early nineteenth century, like Gentleman Jackson, Mendoza and Jim Belcher, with the awe-struck eyes of a boy—a boy, however, who knows what he is writing about in a technical sense, and is able to create the visual background of the period with great skill. "The Croxley Master" is just as good on a smaller scale. The picture of the Master, who might have been one of the great fighters of his time but for an accident which broke his thigh and left one leg shorter than the other, ungainly as a crab in advance or retreat but able to pivot on his bad leg with extraordinary speed, is brilliantly done. The success of these stories emphasizes again that his mastery as a writer was mostly in rendering the external surface of things, whether it was a boxing match or the investigation of a crime.

This exultant acceptance of physical exertion and struggle is to be found, together with a typical love of extrovert characters, in *The Exploits of Brigadier Gerard* (1895) and *The Adventures* that followed in 1903. The Brigadier is an officer in Napoleon's army, a swaggering vain braggart who is also brave, imaginative and resourceful. He is based fairly closely on the Baron de Marbot, whose memoirs show him to have been a real life Gerard so far as boastfulness went, and whose dash and skill were acknowledged even by those who most disliked him. Conan Doyle did not think very much of the Gerard stories. They sprang from his absorption for three years in things Napoleonic, an absorption responsible for *Uncle Bernac* and also for what the author deprecatingly called his little book of soldier stories.

The Gerard stories were probably written as a relaxation from what Conan Doyle thought of as his serious historical fiction, but they have the life and verve that is missing in *The White Company* and *Sir Nigel*. Perhaps it is an exaggeration to say, as one critic does, that he never wrote anything else as good as these tales, but they do show what he could achieve in the way of characterization. Gerard, who reveals occasional traces of Conan Doyle's old friend Dr Budd, was the kind of character he could perfectly understand. All Gerard's qualities show upon the surface. From his boastfulness and courage, his unquenchable self-satisfaction and its frequent humiliation, his disastrous mistakes and adroit recoveries from them, there is built a comic character who is still not absurd. It would be too much to call Gerard one of the great comic characters of literature, but on his own level he is unmatchable. A typical passage is that in which the French commander in Portugal sends for Gerard, and asks him to undertake a special mission:

"Colonel Etienne Gerard," said he, "I have always heard that you are a very gallant and enterprising officer."

It was not for me to confirm such a report, and yet it would be folly to deny it, so I clinked my spurs together and saluted.

"You are also an excellent rider."

I admitted it.

"And the best swordsman in the six brigades of light cavalry."

Massena was famous for the accuracy of his information.

"How the Brigadier Slew the Fox", from which that passage comes, also suggests the flavour of the tales. Gerard gets lost behind the British lines, and finds himself involved in a fox hunt. ("Behind the lines of Torres Vedras these mad Englishmen made the fox-chase three days in the week.") He steals a horse and joins the hunt, seeing in it a chance of escape, but he becomes intoxicated with the pleasure of the chase. Unaware that the fox when caught is always left to be killed by the hounds, he rides ahead of the huntsman with the dogs ("One or two may have been hurt, but what would you have? The egg must be broken for the omelette"), and kills the fox with his sabre. He interprets the anger of the hunters behind him as enthusiasm ("They are not really such a phlegmatic race, the English. A gallant deed in war or in sport will always warm their hearts"), and escapes to the French lines. Most of the stories are anecdotes like this one, but they are marvellously well told, with a humour and good humour that carries a reader along. Brigadier Gerard is, after Holmes and Watson, Conan Doyle's most successful literary creation. He was put on the stage in 1910.

(iii) *The Science Fiction.* This was a development that came late in Conan Doyle's writing career, and is represented by three novels, *The Lost World* (1912), *The Poison Belt* (1913) and *The Maracot Deep* (1929), as well as some short stories. The first, and much the best, of these novels is about a journey to Amazonia, where Professor Challenger claims to have traced some prehistoric animals still living on a great

'The Monster' from the sketchbook of Maple White, one of the characters in *The Lost World.*

EDITED AND ARRANGED BY

A. CONAN DOYLE

AUTHOR OF " MICAH CLARKE," ETC., ETC.

LONDON
LONGMANS, GREEN, AND CO.
1895

Part of the title page from the first
edition of *The Stark Munro Letters*,
Conan Doyle's autobiographical
novel.

Cover of the sixpenny edition of *A Duet With An Occasional Chorus*. Conan Doyle's one attempt at a novel of social manners.

plateau. The irascible Challenger, a figure based on the professor of anatomy at Edinburgh, takes a party of adventurous spirits to look for this lost world. Their adventures are marked by that speculative ingenuity which was one of Conan Doyle's most engaging marks as man and writer, and by an imaginative quality that came into play most fully when he was dealing with scenes outside everyday life. The description of the Amazonian forest obviously owes something to the author's travels, yet it has a kind of spectral quality that removes it from literal reality.

Challenger is also the central figure in *The Poison Belt*, which starts from the not unusual science fiction premise that by some means (in this case the earth moves into a poison belt) human life comes to an end. Challenger gathers together wife and friends in an air-tight shelter, and hopes to survive. Most modern stories would be concerned with what happened to them after the extinction of civilised life, but Conan Doyle was too optimistic a man to consider seriously the end of life as we know it. It turns out that the poison belt through which the earth passed has induced unconsciousness, not death. Everybody wakes up, and life goes on as before. It is a feeble, unsatisfying ending. In *The Maracot Deep* the people of Atlantis are discovered by submarine explorers to have survived the flooding of the city. Wireless, television and nuclear energy are introduced into a story containing many inventive effects, unhappily largely dissipated by the introduction of such unlikely creatures as a giant caterpillar armed with a death ray.

(iv) *Oddities.* The two books that conspicuously fail to fit into any category of Conan Doyle fiction are *The Stark Munro Letters* (1895) and *A Duet, with an Occasional Chorus* (1899). The first of these is a fairly direct autobiographical narrative, put in the form of sixteen letters from the young doctor of the title to a friend in America. The most notable character is Dr Budd, who goes under the name of Cullingworth. The book is far from a perfect novel, but it is infused throughout with Conan Doyle's energetic temperament and over it all broods the spirit of Dr Budd, the badhat whose reckless daring fascinated Conan Doyle to the end of his life.

The book is important to anybody interested in understanding the author's character, and so is *A Duet*, a story which shows a flippancy and

TELEGRAMS:
CROWBOROUGH.
NAT. TEL. No 77.

WINDLESHAM,

CROWBOROUGH,

SUSSEX.

Dear old Chap -

It was a great pleasure to me to
see you all and make dear little
John's acquaintance. His mug will
turn up soon. Sorry about the tennis.
You were handicapped.

I finished my Sherlock today. It is
important as I have now enough for
another book. It is as good as any.

My love to Clara

Your affect brother

A.

Letter from Conan Doyle to his
younger brother Innes. Summer 1913.

lightness unique in Conan Doyle's work. Frank and Maude are to be married, and in the "Overture" they argue about the date. Frank (read Conan Doyle) confesses his lack of prospects. "Position I have none to offer," he says. "What is the exact position of the wife of the assistant-accountant of the Co-operative Insurance Office?" The banns are read, the first presents received—a fish-slice for the groom and another for the bride—the wedding takes place, they honeymoon at the Metropole in Brighton, start housekeeping together, face the prospect of ruin and evade it, end up with the birth of their first child. The book's lightness of tone is not successful, yet the author was not altogether wrong when he wrote to the Ma'am: "My inmost soul tells me that it is not a failure." *A Duet* is a gesture, never repeated, in the direction of a novel of social manners, and as an experiment it is certainly not without interest.

That is the sum of Conan Doyle's activities as a literary man, with the exception of his plays and poems. The published texts of his plays make it clear that he was not a natural dramatist, and the collected poems show that he was a competent maker of verses rather than a poet. Anybody who wants to approach him as a man of letters should read the Sherlock Holmes stories, the major historical novels, the Brigadier Gerard tales, one of the science fiction novels, and a selection of the short stories. Only the scholar will want to go further. Conan Doyle was a skilful writer, with a real gift for narrative, but in the end he was a fine craftsman rather than an artist.

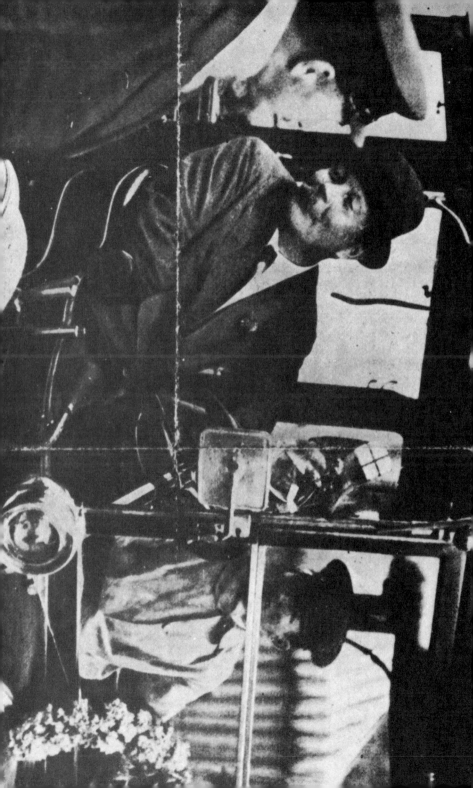

CHAPTER SIX
WARTIME, AND THE LAST YEARS

In 1911 Conan Doyle took part in a motor race called Prince Henry's tour. The Prince was Prussian, the race began in Germany and ended in London after a circular tour of England and Scotland, and fifty British drivers were matched against fifty German. Conan Doyle drove his twenty horse-power Dietrich-Lorraine, and took Jean as a passenger. "It is the reliability of car and man which counts, not speed," he told the Ma'am, and he looked forward to a fine sporting contest.

The race was won by the British team, and Prince Henry presented them with the ivory lady called "Peace" for which they had competed, but Conan Doyle's reaction from what he saw and heard was to sense that war was not far away. He had been accompanied by various young Prussian officers as observers, and more than one of them made the assumption that war between Britain and Germany was inevitable, and welcomed the prospect. He told his brother Innes that he did not like the look of things, and from this time onward he was concerned by the country's unreadiness for war. He exaggerated the power of the airship, but was very perceptive about the threat posed by that comparatively new vessel, the submarine. He wrote a long short story called "Danger", in which Britain's enemy "Norland" had a squad of submarines which ignored the British navy but made merciless attacks on merchant shipping, causing famine and forcing the British Government to sue for peace. Conan Doyle was a strong advocate of the Channel Tunnel, which would serve as a kind of underground railway connecting Britain and France. His warning of the submarine threat was laughed at, and the tunnel was not built, but three years later the German Naval Secretary said that Conan Doyle had been "the only prophet of the present form of economic warfare", submarine attacks on merchant shipping.

This seemed to him an issue so overwhelmingly more important than any other that he was impatient with most projects for reform. He detested the suffragette movement, and on arrival in America in the spring of 1914 rashly said in an interview that he feared the suffragettes might be lynched. One paper's headline read: "Sherlock's Here: Expects Lynching of 'Wild Women'." The suffragettes retorted by putting vitriol through the letter-box of the house in Crowborough to which he had moved in 1909. Conan Doyle's opposition to the suffragettes was based on a belief that it was pointless for women to have the vote, but he felt also that

all live, dear, from "Ole Bill"

'Ole Bill'—Private Arthur Conan
Doyle of the Crowborough Company
of the 6th Royal Sussex Volunteer
Regiment, 1914.

TELEGRAMS:
CROWBOROUGH.
NAT. TEL. No. 77.

WINDLESHAM,
CROWBOROUGH,
SUSSEX.

My dear boy

K has stuck up our Civilian
movement. I am convinced he does
not appreciate its force or scope or how
it would focus his material & put it
under his hand for recruiting. I am
going up today to see if anything can
be done. It is deplorable. We have
had 1000 applications for particulars
from every corner of Eyland.

I want your advice. Do you
think it would be a good thing for me
to apply for a Captaincy (very senior)
in the new Army. I am quite a good
drill, though I say so, being so amenable.

I would soon master the rest. I thought they will have lots of subalterns from O.T.C but not many senior regimental officers. If I join at 55 I would shame others into doing the same. Personally I should love the work & would try to be subordinate — which is my failing. I have drawn up my application but wont send it in before the weekend. Or can I serve my country better in any other way?

Malcolm is in Belgium & I fear in a post of great danger. Wood at Dover. K in Chelsea sleeping in a haystack.

Your loving brother

A

In an undated letter to his brother Innes in 1914, Conan Doyle complains about Kitchener's attempts to prevent him forming a civilian volunteer force.

their activities were monstrous and unwomanly. On the other hand he was sympathetic to reform of the Divorce Law, by which a husband could obtain a divorce on the ground of his wife's adultery, but a wife had to prove not only adultery but also brutality or desertion. He was president of the Divorce Law Reform Society, and frequently spoke and wrote for reform. But all such activities were submerged with the declaration of war in August, 1914.

He said afterwards that the War was the physical climax of his life, a remarkable statement when one remembers that he was fifty-five when it began. In a personal sense he certainly enjoyed himself immensely during these four years. Within a day or two he had organized in Crowborough a civilian group called the Volunteers. He received requests for their rules and methods from twelve hundred towns and villages, but within a few weeks the force was disbanded by order of the War Office. It was replaced by an official body which grew to 200,000 men, and Conan Doyle served in it as a private during the whole of the War. Many of the men in his company were in their fifties or even older, but "it was quite usual for us to march from Crowborough to Frant, with our rifles and equipment, to drill for a long hour in a heavy marshy field, and then to march back, singing all the way. It would be a good 14 miles, apart from the drill."

This, however, was nothing like enough for him. He wanted to see action, and volunteered for the Army, but of course was not accepted. He peppered the War Office with ideas, some of them both ingenious and practical. Warships carried few boats because they were easily inflammable, with the consequence that the seamen had little chance of survival if the ship was torpedoed. Conan Doyle suggested the development of india rubber boats, and although this was not accepted he was partly responsible for the hurried ordering of inflatable rubber collars which seamen carried in their pockets. His campaign for body armour, in the form of breastplates issued to troops in the front line seems equally sensible, but it was rejected. At the Ministry of Munitions he was told: "Sir Arthur, there is no use arguing here, for there is no one in the building who does not know that you are right."

But his principal occupation during these four years was that of propagandist. Within a month of the War's beginning he had written a pamphlet called "To Arms", and he quickly set to work on a history

Battle of the Somme, July, 1916.
Conan Doyle's eldest son Kingsley was badly wounded there, later dying of pneumonia.

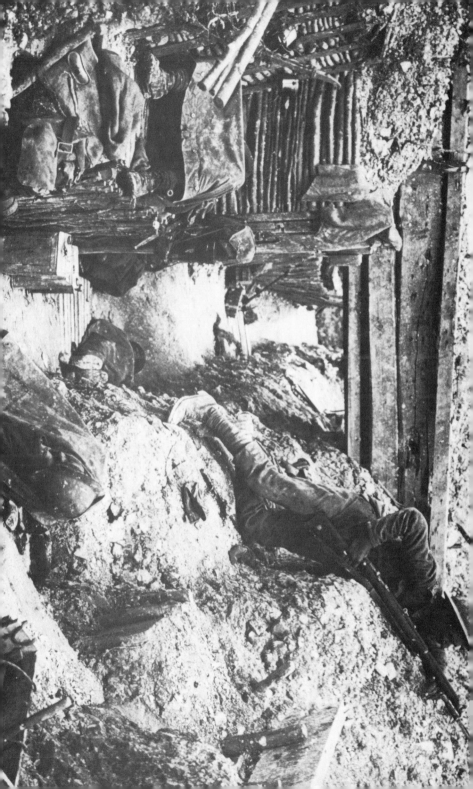

called "The British Campaign in France and Flanders". He was in close touch with several of the British commanders, and accepted most of what they told him, so that the work he produced cannot be taken as a serious history. Conan Doyle had a passion for justice, but unless he thought that wrong had been done, he was in the ordinary affairs of life wholly on the side of authority. He also had a deep respect for the military caste, feeling that their code of values was very much his own. "I have had great luck," he wrote exultantly to Innes. "I have Smith-Dorrien's diaries and am promised Haig's, so on the top of Bulfin's, I am pretty well informed. I shall now do a worthy book and it may well be my Magnum Opus, for the subject will make it illustrious." He was sadly deceived, as he was often deceived about the value of his own work. He was so closely in touch with commanders, and had so much respect for them, that his history of the British campaign is one of the least valuable things he wrote. His archives contain letters from forty-eight Generals, and at one time he is said to have received five letters from commanders by every post.

He was not content to sit at home, even though that involved marches

8-inch howitzers in action at the Battle of the Somme, August 1916.

George V, French President Poincaré
and Sir Douglas Haig (*r. to l.*) at
Montreuil, 7th August, 1918.

from Crowborough to Frant. In 1916 he accepted a mission to "write up" the Italian army, taking a look at the British front in France on the way. As a deputy-lieutenant of Surrey he had the right to wear a uniform when with troops, and his tailor "rigged me up in a wondrous khaki garb which was something between that of a Colonel and a Brigadier, with silver roses instead of stars or crosses upon the shoulder-straps". He felt like an impostor but looked impressive, especially when wearing his South African medals, and he was treated everywhere with respect. He went to France on a destroyer instead of a steamer in the company of General Robertson, then Chief of Staff, and met several Generals. He also saw Innes, who was now a Colonel. Haig appeared to him to have some of the traits of Wellington, and he was impressed both by Army organization and by the enthusiasm of the soldiers. Even "the half-mad cranks whose absurd consciences" made them object to killing, seemed to him to be turning into men. "I saw a batch of them, neurotic and largely bespectacled, but working with a will by the roadside." The military jingo and the man of sensibility were strangely blended in Conan Doyle.

Conan Doyle at the Italian Front, 1916.

On then to the Italian front, where his hosts tried without success to keep him out of harm's way. His party was shelled, nearly hit, and had to retire without reaching their objective. He made sheaves of notes about the Italian soldiers, wrote them up on his return, and was told that his visit had been an unqualified success. Later he was invited to breakfast by Lloyd George, who had replaced Asquith as Prime Minister. Conan Doyle, who fetched the bacon and eggs while Lloyd George poured the tea, listened to some severe criticism of the recently-dead Kitchener, and heard that the soldiers always obstructed new ideas. A few weeks before the War ended he was invited by the Australian Government to see their section of the line, and got some glimpses of the vital battle of St Quentin.

It seems fair enough for Conan Doyle to have called these years the physical climax of his life. The marching and drilling at home, the visits to various fronts, the sense of being at the heart of historical events, all these allowed him to indulge his boyish love of adventure. But the War and its aftermath also brought him the deepest grief. First his wife's brother was killed, then two nephews and other friends and relatives. And then Kingsley, the only son of his first marriage, and his much-loved brother Innes, died within a few weeks of each other. Kingsley had been badly wounded on the Somme, and died of pneumonia in October, 1918. In the following February Innes, now a Brigadier-General, also went down with pneumonia and died. Conan Doyle said and wrote little of this, but the blows must have been hard, harder even than the death of the Ma'am two years later. He had perhaps been closer to her than to any other human being, including his wives, but the Ma'am was in her eighties. Innes had always been very distinctly Arthur's younger brother, and Kingsley was only twenty-six.

Although these deaths were not responsible for his belief in the validity of spiritualism, they must have added force and feeling to it. The interest in the occult derived from his Irish forebears, and evident in his father's drawings and paintings, had remained constant throughout his life. It is the basis for a number of stories, and once he emerged from the brief agnosticism of his youth, he had speculated frequently on the nature of life after death. At the beginning of the War he was still no more than a sympathizer, but as he said in *The New Revelation* (1918) all the wartime deaths and suffering convinced him that those we love must continue to exist after death. In the spring of 1916 he made a note in his commonplace book: "The breath of the Spirit can blow through this room tonight as easily as it once did through the upper Chamber in Jerusalem. God did not die two thousand years ago. He is here and now."

Before the end of the year he announced his conversion in the psychic magazine *Light*. A little later he said that he was in touch with thirteen mothers who were corresponding through spiritualistic mediums with their dead sons. He put the essential nature of his belief very clearly.

> The physical basis of all psychic belief is that the soul is a complete duplicate of the body, resembling it in the smallest particular, although constructed in some far more tenuous material.

It was vital to Britain's survival that the War should be won, but he thought it just as vital that humanity should recognize the truth of the new revelation. His first shots in the religious battle were fired in October, 1917, in one of the most critical periods of the War, when he gave lectures in Bradford and London. These were the first of many talks, books and articles. During one lecture tour he received a telegram sent by his daughter Mary giving the news of Kingsley's death. He went on to give the lecture, saying that Kingsley would have wished it, and that it was better so.

In the course of these years he visited almost every town in Britain, finding, as he said, critical but attentive audiences. Perhaps people came to hear the creator of Sherlock Holmes rather than from an interest in life after death, but if so he did not care. In 1920 he went with Jean and his family to spread the word in Australia, and then a couple of years later made a lecture tour in the United States. Other European countries received the message, and in 1928 he went to South Africa, Rhodesia and Kenya. He had suffered heart palpitations occasionally even during the War years, and in the twenties he had more than one heart attack, but he ignored the doctors who told him to rest. There were more lectures to be given, more books to be written. In 1926 he published a psychic adventure story called *The Land of Mist*, and also a two volume *History of Spiritualism*. In these years he spent a quarter of a million pounds in advancing the spiritualist cause.

He insisted that he was by no means uncritical in considering reports of what had been achieved through mediums and in assessing results obtained by automatic writing and spirit photography, but to those who were not believers many of his activities and statements seemed ridiculous. He also met with hostility from some Christians, who felt that his certainty about physical existence after death was blasphemous. A Roman Catholic convert wrote to say that he was a disgusting beast who should be horsewhipped for his filthy caricatures of Jesus Christ. Conan Doyle replied that he was relieved by the letter. "It is only your approval that could in any way annoy me." Two aspects of his spiritualistic activities generally ignored by biographers show the extremes to which he was led.

One of these was the discovery by two young girls in the North of

The Doyle family en route to America in 1923: (*l. to r.*) Denis, Lady Conan Doyle, Jean, C.D., and Adrian.

IRIS AND THE DANCING GNOME.
(An untouched enlargement from the original negative.)
THIS PICTURE AND THE EVEN MORE EXTRAORDINARY
ONE OF THE FAIRIES ON PAGE 465 ARE THE TWO
MOST ASTOUNDING PHOTOGRAPHS EVER PUBLISHED.
HOW THEY WERE TAKEN IS FULLY DESCRIBED IN SIR
A. CONAN DOYLE'S AMAZING ARTICLE.

(See page 466.)

ALICE AND THE FAIRIES.

ALICE STANDING BEHIND THE BANKS OF THE BECK, WITH FAIRIES DANCING BEFORE HER.
SHE IS LOOKING ACROSS AT HER PLAYMATE IRIS, TO INTIMATE THAT THE TIME HAD COME TO
TAKE THE PHOTOGRAPH.

(An untouched enlargement from the original negative.)

Some of the photographic 'evidence' that convinced
Conan Doyle that fairies actually existed. In 1922 he
published a book about his beliefs called *The Coming of the
Fairies.*

England that there were literally fairies at the bottom of their garden. Photographs of the fairies were taken, and although these look most unconvincing in reproduction, Conan Doyle's enthusiastic acceptance of them led him so far as to write a book called *The Coming of the Fairies* (1922). He was undisturbed by the ridicule with which the book was greeted. The other indication of his credulity is more personal. The Ma'am had always disbelieved in spiritualism and disapproved of her son's interest in it, and Jean too had disliked his concern with a subject she felt to be "uncanny and dangerous". The death of Jean's brother Malcolm in the War, however, changed her feelings, and in 1921 she was suddenly given what her husband called "the gift of inspired writing". Thereafter direct spirit communications came to the family circle. In the following year an Arabian spirit guide named Pheneas came through for the first time, and took control so that the writing changed to "semi-trance inspirational talking". By this means it was possible to converse not only with Malcolm Leckie, but with Kingsley, Innes and E. W. Hornung.

The level of communication, whether by automatic writing or through Pheneas the Arab, was always simple and on occasion almost infantile. "I am so glad to be here, Arthur, this is wonderful," said Hornung, who in life had been a sceptic. Asked whether the work he did on the other side was literary he said, "Yes, of a kind", but did not condescend to detail. The Ma'am came on and said that she should have trusted Arthur's judgement. Everything about the other world was beautiful, although nothing was specific. "I never saw any home on earth to compare with our home here", was a common phrase to come from the spirits. John Delane, the great editor of *The Times* (whose very name, as Conan Doyle said, was unknown to the medium Jean), came through especially to give the assurance that "a pleasant home is being prepared for you".

One would have thought that somebody with Conan Doyle's commonsense would have been sceptical of such messages, and might have thought that the spirits should be silent if they had nothing more significant to say. Once he had been converted, however, scepticism was abandoned, and he accepted the messages—which can be found in *Pheneas Speaks* (1927)—without question. In his autobiography Conan Doyle listed his own experiences, which included grasping materialized

A faked photograph of ectoplasm coming from the mouth of a medium. The manifestation is supposedly of a dead girl.

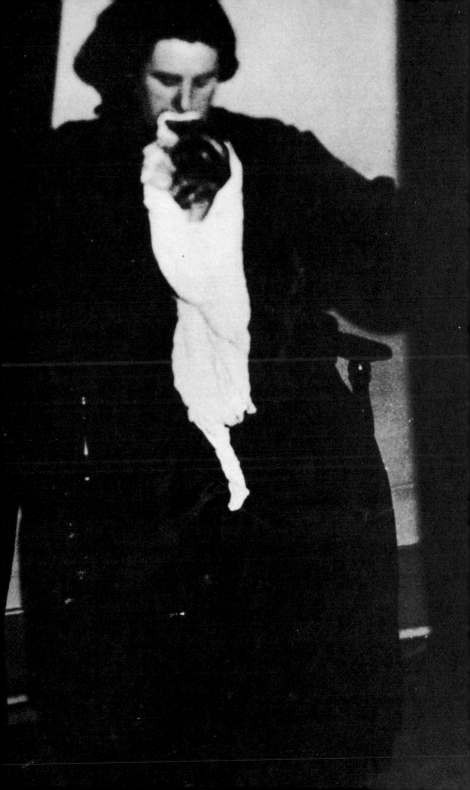

hands, smelling "the peculiar ozone-like smell of ectoplasm", seeing dead people glimmer on an untouched photographic plate, watching heavy articles swimming in the air, and reading books written by unlettered mediums which might have been the work of great thinkers and scholars, as well as receiving "through the hand of my own wife, notebooks full of information which was utterly beyond her ken". He seems never to have asked himself why figures from the other world should have manifested themselves in such curious ways and places, nor to have reflected on the fact that many of these effects are the standard trappings of cheating mediums, and that others may be explained by telepathy. What would Sherlock Holmes have said, one sadly asks? The reply must surely be that he would have said that there are no limits to human credulity.

Spiritualism occupied the major part of his energies in the years after the War, but there was plenty left over for other things. He still wrote books and stories, including a few about Sherlock Holmes; he took an active part, as already mentioned, in the final push to clear Oscar Slater's name; and he was fascinated, as he had always been, in recent scientific developments. He saw the blossoming of wireless sets, so that they became a means of entertainment and information for the many instead of a scientific invention for the few, and he was delighted by the increased potentialities of the internal combustion engine. In 1929 he was taken round Brooklands racing track at 70 miles an hour.

He also had business interests, which remained in the background of his life, but were nevertheless important to him. He believed that "a man should know all sides of life, and he has missed a very essential side if he has not played his part in commerce". He was not altogether a successful business man, making heavy losses on a manufacturing plant in Birmingham, and in an attempt to mine coal in Kent. He went down a thousand feet to see "with my own eyes that the coal was *in situ*", but it proved to be incombustible, and at a shareholders' dinner which was to be cooked by local coal, it proved necessary to send out and buy something which would burn. Some of his business adventures went better, and in the nineteen twenties he congratulated himself that he had been for many years chairman of one famous firm and a director of another. He was as busy in this decade as he had been throughout his adult life.

Yet in spite of all this, the world after the War was deeply alien to him.

His writing and his beliefs about the conduct of life belonged to an earlier age, and the War wiped away such attitudes so that those who emerged from it often felt that they were living on another planet. As a novelist Conan Doyle had been out of place, and had looked old-fashioned, even among the great Edwardians, Wells, Bennett and Shaw. In spite of his interest in new inventions, he was conservative by nature as well as by political belief, and the Socialism of Wells and Shaw was anathema to him. The post-war British writers, such as Aldous Huxley and D. H. Lawrence, with their cynicism about the Empire and their assumption of sexual freedom must have seemed to be jeering at things he held sacred, and if he read James Joyce's *Ulysses* he must have been disgusted by its verbal explicitness.

These writers reflected a general attitude among young people after the War. Conan Doyle had standards of behaviour that were outraged by what he saw around him in the Twenties. Women smoked in public, wore short skirts and went out looking for jobs. Young men no longer aspired to a healthy mind in a healthy body, and no longer behaved with decorum. Does all this sound absurd? It must be remembered that he was a man altogether opposed to women being given the vote, and a man who struck his son because he said that a woman was ugly. In a political sense also the decade provided an unpleasant shock to his conservatism when a Labour Government took office in 1924, for he had always regarded Socialism as both unEnglish and undesirable. In this new world he was an anachronism, and he was too intelligent not to know it.

Yet a man so pugnacious was bound to struggle against attitudes which seemed to him to spring from insanity or wickedness. As early as 1912 he had noted in his journal the degeneration of modern art. The Pre-Raphaelite painters (like Rossetti and Burne-Jones) and the French symbolist poets (like Mallarmé and Verlaine) seemed to him queer, but the post-Impressionists (Picasso and Braque) and the Italian Futurists with their idea of reproducing movement in painting, appeared to him merely mad. "One should put one's shoulder to the door and keep out insanity all one can", and when a bas-relief by Epstein was unveiled in Hyde Park he was one of the signatories of a letter demanding the removal of this piece of "artistic anarchy". It is sad that the man who had been able to put aside personal feeling in an attempt to save the life of Roger

The offending Epstein bas-relief in
London's Hyde Park, which Conan
Doyle petitioned to have removed.

The frontispiece of *Three of Them*, featuring Conan Doyle's children: Billie (Jean), Dimples (Adrian), and Laddie (Denis).

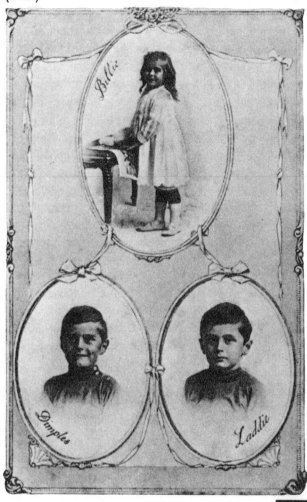

Their cousin John Doyle. The four children played together as 'The Leatherskin Tribe'.

Casement should have been so intolerant in relation to art, but Conan Doyle identified such art with things that he found abhorrent in life. He no doubt linked what he regarded as artistic anarchy with the Russian Revolution of 1917, which seemed to him an almost inconceivable event. "It was as though a robust man had suddenly softened into liquid putrescence before one's eyes," he wrote, and he believed that in a short time the Communist regime must be overthrown, and the robust and healthy Russian man reappear.

The years after the War, then, must in some ways have been unhappy, and it may be that his deepening immersion in spiritualism sprang in part from a feeling that only by conversion to spiritualist beliefs could humanity be saved from one of those eras like that of the French Revolution, which he saw as odious in themselves even though they might contain the seeds of something new and better. He struggled on in 1929 through shortness of breath and heart attacks, and insisted on speaking at Armistice meetings, even though he had been told that to speak might mean his death. He recovered after being confined to his room for some weeks, and in the spring began to deal again with his correspondence and to learn the art of painting. Then he had another heart attack and in the morning

Attack on the Officers' School in Great Grebetskayia Street, Petrograd, in January, 1918. The Russian Revolution seemed to Conan Doyle an appalling, almost inconceivable event.

of July 7, 1930, after being shifted from his bed to a big basket-chair facing the bedroom windows, he died.

What should one say as a valediction? The historical romances by which he expected to be remembered seem now as old as out-of-date clothes, and it is not likely that they will ever be popular again. What he would have called the tide of artistic anarchy has washed away most of the art and literature he valued, and the world of British power and influence that he thought would be eternal has gone for ever. Yet a great deal remains of him, both as writer and man. The Sherlock Holmes stories will be read as long as humanity keeps its love for puzzles. Some of the other tales, in particular the Gerard stories, will last while we retain our feeling for tales of adventure zestfully and skilfully told.

And his behaviour as a man was throughout his life almost wholly admirable. The indignation he felt at official cruelty or neglect, and his struggles to obtain justice for men personally uncongenial to him, show him as a man of an integrity rare in his own or any time. He lived by the code of the period in which he was brought up, and never looked far outside it, but within that code he tried always to behave honourably. He made a drawing not long before his death called "The Old Horse", showing himself as a weary but willing animal, pulling along a cart piled high by "Life Work Carriage Co" with cases labelled sport and business, and others bearing the names of novels, histories, psychic research, Sherlock Holmes. But such a simile does him less than justice. A French journalist once called him the good giant, and the phrase fits him perfectly. His aesthetic perceptions were limited, as those of giants are apt to be, but this huge man knew his own strength in both a physical and a moral sense, and tried always to use it for the good of humanity. In his work and in his personality he is the ideal representative of the Victorian era to which he belonged.

This bibliography is divided into six sections for ease of reference. The dates refer to book publication, something which is often not identical with first publication, since so much of Conan Doyle's work appeared in serial form in magazines. Pamphlets have not been included, nor have the published texts of plays. Many of the short stories have been published in omnibus volumes, with different titles from those given here.

Sherlock Holmes Novels and Stories

A Study in Scarlet	1888
The Sign of the Four (later The Sign of Four)	1890
The Adventures of Sherlock Holmes	1892
The Memoirs of Sherlock Holmes	1894
The Hound of the Baskervilles	1902
The Return of Sherlock Holmes	1905
The Valley of Fear	1915
His Last Bow	1917
The Case-Book of Sherlock Holmes	1927

Fiction, excluding short stories

Micah Clarke	1889
The Mystery of Cloomber	1889
The Firm of Girdlestone	1890
The White Company	1891
The Doings of Raffles Haw	1892
The Refugees	1893
The Parasite	1894
The Stark Munro Letters	1895
Rodney Stone	1896
Uncle Bernac	1897
The Tragedy of the Korosko	1898
A Duet with an Occasional Chorus	1899
Sir Nigel	1906
The Lost World	1912
The Poison Belt	1913
The Land of Mist	1926
The Maracot Deep	1929

Short Story Collections

Mysteries and Adventures	1889
The Captain of the Pole-Star	1890
Round the Red Lamp	1894
The Exploits of Brigadier Gerard	1896
The Green Flag	1900
The Adventures of Gerard	1903
Round the Fire Stories	1908
The Last Galley	1911
Danger!	1918
Tales of Adventure and Medical Life	1922

Histories

The Great Boer War	1900
The British Campaign in France and Flanders	1916-1919

Autobiography and Belles-Lettres

Through the Magic Door	1907
Three of Them	1923
Memories and Adventures	1924

Poems

Songs of Action	1898
Songs of the Road	1911
The Guards Came Through	1919

Spiritualism

The New Revelation	1918
Vital Message	1919
The Wanderings of a Spiritualist	1921
The Coming of the Fairies	1922
Our American Adventure	1923
Our Second American Adventure	1924
The History of Spiritualism (2 Volumes)	1926
Pheneas Speaks	1927
Our African Winter	1929
The Edge of the Unknown	1930

SOME BOOKS ABOUT CONAN DOYLE:

Conan Doyle—His Life and Art
by Hesketh Pearson (Methuen, 1943)
The Life of Sir Arthur Conan Doyle
by John Dickson Carr (John Murray, 1949)
Conan Doyle by Pierre Nordon
(translated by Francis Partridge—John Murray, 1966)

CHRONOLOGY

1859 Arthur Conan Doyle born May 22 in Edinburgh, the second child of Charles Doyle and Mary Foley.

1868 Sent away to Hodder, the preparatory school for Stonyhurst—a Catholic public school in Lancashire run by Jesuits.

1870 Enters Stonyhurst and remains there for five years, excelling at cricket and displaying early signs of literary talent.

1874 Visits London and stays with his uncle, Richard Doyle. Sees Henry Irving in *Hamlet*.

1875 Doyle passes matriculation examination with honours, and spends year at Jesuit school at Feldkirch, in Austria, to improve his German.

1876 He decides to become a doctor and enrols at Edinburgh University. While there he meets Dr Joseph Bell, on whom Sherlock Holmes is largely based. Also the anatomist Professor Rutherford, later a model for Professor Challenger.

1878 Takes part-time job assisting a Dr Richardson in Sheffield—the first of several doctoring jobs while a student.

1879 Charles Doyle goes into a nursing home. Early Conan Doyle stories published anonymously.

1880 Signs on as ship's doctor with Arctic whaler and leaves on seven-month voyage. Initial interest in spiritualism and the paranormal.

1881 Doyle graduates as Bachelor of Medicine. Makes second voyage as ship's doctor, this time on a cargo steamer heading for West Africa. Nearly dies of fever en route.

1882 Tells family he has lost his Catholic faith. Accepts offer to join medical practice of former fellow-student Dr Budd, in Plymouth. Becomes concerned about Budd's unorthodox and unscrupulous methods and leaves to set up his own practice in Southsea, a suburb of Portsmouth.

1883 The prestigious *Cornhill* magazine publishes short story based on *Marie Celeste* mystery.

1884 Begins a novel, *The Firm of Girdlestone*, eventually published in 1890.

1885 Marries Louise Hawkins, sister of a patient.

1887 First Sherlock Holmes story, *A Study in Scarlet*, published in *Beeton's Christmas Annual*.

1889 Daughter Mary Louise born. *Micah Clarke* published. Also the second Holmes mystery, *The Sign of the Four*.

1890 Doyle visits Berlin to investigate bacteriologist Robert Koch's claim to have found a cure for tuberculosis. Correctly rejects claim. *The White Company*.

1891 Abandons Southsea practice and goes to Vienna with Louise to study eye medicine, with a view to specializing in it. Plan falls through and Doyle writes book, *The Doings of Raffles Haw*, instead. Returns to London and opens practice in Devonshire Place, but soon decides to give up medicine altogether and write full-time. Six Sherlock Holmes stories appear in *Strand Magazine*.

1892 The Doyles go to Norway with writer Jerome K. Jerome and Conan Doyle skis for the first time. Shortly after he helps introduce the sport in Switzerland. Son Kingsley born.

1893 Charles Doyle dies. Louise falls ill with tuberculosis and is given only a few months to live. Conan Doyle takes her to Switzerland for a cure. The *Strand* publish the death of Sherlock Holmes in 'The Final Problem'. Doyle joins the Psychical Research Society.

1894 Lecture tour in America great success. Play *Waterloo* performed in London with Henry Irving.

1895 Doyle buys land in Hindhead to build house on, having been advised that the therapeutic Surrey air would help Louise. He takes her to Eygpt for the winter. *The Stark Munro Letters*.

1896 The Doyles travel up the Nile to the Sudan, later the background for his novel, *The Tragedy of the Korosko*. Fighting breaks out between the British and the Dervishes, and Doyle acts briefly as war correspondent for *The Westminster Gazette*. *The Exploits of Brigadier Gerard. Rodney Stone*.

1897 Doyle meets and falls in love with Jean Leckie, later to become his wife. *Uncle Bernac*.

1899 Second Boer War begins. Doyle volunteers for the army but is not accepted. *A Duet with an Occasional Chorus*.

1900 Joins hospital unit as doctor and sails for South Africa in February. Works there under appalling conditions and visits the front. Returns to England in July and writes *The Great Boer War*. Then *The War in South Africa: Its Causes and Conduct* in response to strong criticism of the British treatment of the Boers. Stands as Unionist candidate in Edinburgh at the General Election, but fails to win seat.

1902 Conan Doyle is knighted. Sherlock Holmes returns in *The Hound of the Baskervilles*, but in a story dated before his 'death'.

1903 Persuaded by lucrative American offer to bring Holmes back properly. The first of the new stories appears in the *Strand*. *The Adventures of Gerard*.

1904 Doyle takes 7 wickets for 51 runs for the MCC in cricket match against Cambridgeshire.

1906 Stands unsuccessfully as Unionist candidate in Hawick at General Election. Doyle takes up the cause of George Edalji, unjustly imprisoned in 1903. Becomes involved in Divorce Law Reform Movement. Louise Doyle dies. *Sir Nigel*.

1907 George Edalji released. Conan Doyle marries Jean Leckie. *Through the Magic Door*.

1909 Doyle writes *The Crime of the Congo* to expose the barbaric cruelties practised on natives in the Belgian Congo by the trading companies. Son Denis born.

1910 Becomes interested in the case of Oscar Slater, a German Jew accused of murder in Scotland. Fights his cause for the next 17 years until Slater's release in 1927. Another son, Adrian, born.

1911 Takes part in Prince Henry's Tour, an Anglo-German motor race won by the British.

1912 Publishes *The Case of Oscar Slater*. Introduces Professor Challenger in *The Lost World*. Daughter Lena Jean born.

1913 *The Poison Belt*.

1914 Outbreak of World War I. Doyle forms local volunteer force, later replaced by official body in which he serves as private. Writes rallying pamphlet *To Arms!*

1915 Begins 6-volume history of *The British Campaign in France and Flanders*, completed in 1920. *The Valley of Fear*.

1916 Doyle visits the British, French and Italian fronts. Meets Haig and other Generals. Unsuccessfully appeals for the reprieve of Sir Roger Casement, sentenced to death for treason. Announces his conversion to spiritualism in the psychic magazine *Light*.

1917 *His Last Bow*.

1918 Under fire while visiting Australian troops at the battle of St. Quentin. Kingsley Doyle dies of pneumonia after having been wounded at the Somme. Conan Doyle's first book about spiritualism, *The New Revelation*, is published.

1919 Brother Innes dies of pneumonia. *The Vital Message.*

1920 Takes family to Australia to spread the word of spiritualism.

1921 Doyle's mother dies. Jean Conan Doyle discovers an ability to act as a medium for trance-writing. *The Wanderings of a Spiritualist.*

1922 Lecture tour of America. Conan Doyle declares his belief in fairies in *The Coming of the Fairies*. First 'appearance' of the Arabian spirit guide Pheneas, resulting in trance-speaking and communication with dead members of the Doyle family and others.

1923 Returns to America and Canada. *Our American Adventure.*

1924 *Our Second American Adventure. Memories and Adventures.*

1925 Doyle presides over International Spiritualistic Congress in Paris.

1926 Publishes 2-volume *History of Spiritualism* and *The Land of Mist*, a Professor Challenger adventure with a spiritualist theme.

1927 Oscar Slater freed but falls out with Doyle. *The Case-Book of Sherlock Holmes*, the last stories; and *Pheneas Speaks*, messages from the beyond.

1928 The Doyles go to South Africa, Kenya and Rhodesia. Jean Conan Doyle evokes the spirits of Cecil Rhodes and Paul Kruger at a seance.

1929 Visits to Scandanavia and Holland. Doyle returns exhausted and has heart attack, but insists on speaking at Armistice Day meetings as planned. Subsequently confined to his room for many weeks. *The Maracot Deep. Our African Winter.*

1930 Death of Sir Arthur Conan Doyle on July 7. *The Edge of the Unknown.*

LIST OF ILLUSTRATIONS

Picture research by Illustration Research Service. Photographs of all books out of copyright by John Freeman.

INDEX

Sherlock Holmes short stories:

Collected Sherlock Holmes stories:

Sherlock Holmes novels:

Historical novels and stories:

The Mysterious Library offers enduring works of reference, biography, and fiction covering the entire spectrum of crime and supense literature.

Eric Ambler: HERE LIES: AN AUTOBIOGRAPHY
The Edgar Award-winning autobiography of the man Graham Greene called "our greatest thriller writer." ILLUSTRATED.
$8.95

Robert Barnard: A TALENT TO DECEIVE: AN APPRECIATION OF AGATHA CHRISTIE
The definitive critical study and celebration of the lady whose name is synonymous with mystery, by the distinguished mystery author.
$8.95

Raymond Chandler: RAYMOND CHANDLER'S UNKNOWN THRILLER: THE SCREENPLAY OF "PLAYBACK"
An entirely new story—in the form of a never-produced screenplay—by one of the 20th century's most influential authors.
$9.95

Carroll John Daly: THE ADVENTURES OF SATAN HALL (A *Dime Detective Book*)
A series of 1930s novellas featuring "The Man Police and Gangdom Alike Feared," by the most popular writer of pulp detective stories.
$8.95

Norbert Davis: THE ADVENTURES OF MAX LATIN (A *Dime Detective Book*)
Novellas from the 1930s and '40s featuring a most unusual private eye, by one of the most talented of the pulp writers. With an introduction by John D. MacDonald.
$8.95

Patricia Highsmith: THE ANIMAL-LOVER'S BOOK OF BEASTLY MURDER
A series of extraordinary murder tales, each featuring a protagonist who is not man but beast.
$8.95

Patricia Highsmith: LITTLE TALES OF MISOGYNY
Seventeen bizarre, sophisticated, ironic, and humorous stories about women who destroy their men and women who destroy themselves.
$8.95

Patricia Highsmith: SLOWLY, SLOWLY IN THE WIND
A dozen short stories which explore the guilt—or lack of it—in
their characters, and justice—or the lack of it—in their world.
$8.95

Peter Lovesey: BUTCHERS AND OTHER STORIES OF CRIME
The award-winning author's first collection of short stories. "One of
the most amusing, original, and surprising writers in the crime
field."—*Police*
$9.95

Gregory Mcdonald, ed. LAST LAUGHS:
THE 1986 MYSTERY WRITERS OF AMERICA ANTHOLOGY
Fourteen unusual mystery stories which prove that even crime may
be humorous.
$8.95

Frederick Nebel: THE ADVENTURES OF CARDIGAN
(A *Dime Detective Book*)
A series of 1930s private eye novellas by one of the finest
practitioners of the Dashiell Hammett school of pulp writing.
$9.95

William F. Nolan: THE BLACK MASK BOYS: MASTERS IN THE
HARD-BOILED SCHOOL OF DETECTIVE FICTION
The story of the men who invented and refined the hard-boiled
form and created the fabled *Black Mask* magazine.
$8.95

Bill Pronzini: GUN IN CHEEK
A delightful exploration of "alternative" crime fiction—the most
inept writing in the genre.
$9.95

Bill Pronzini: SON OF GUN IN CHEEK
Taken with its companion volume, this study provides a hilarious
crash course in the worst crime fiction of the 20th century.
$8.95

Robert J. Randisi, ed.: THE EYES HAVE IT
The first anthology from the Private Eye Writers of America,
bringing together the most distinguished practitioners of the genre.
$8.95

Robert J. Randisi, ed.: MEAN STREETS
The second anthology from the Private Eye Writers of America
continues to showcase the work of today's best hard-boiled writers.
$8.95

Hank Searls: THE ADVENTURES OF MIKE BLAIR
(A *Dime Detective* Book)
A collection of hard-boiled novellas which provide a fascinating
look at the pulp apprenticeship of one of today's most
accomplished suspense authors.
$8.95

Ralph B. Sipper: ROSS MACDONALD'S INWARD JOURNEY
A collection of essays by and about one of the greatest of
modern-day mystery writers. ILLUSTRATED.
$8.95

Vincent Starrett: THE PRIVATE LIFE OF SHERLOCK HOLMES
Written by the most distinguished of all Sherlockian scholars, this
is the first comprehensive biography of the world's most famous
detective. ILLUSTRATED.
$8.95

Julian Symons: CONAN DOYLE: PORTRAIT OF AN ARTIST
A brilliantly concise and readable introduction to the man and his
work, by the well-known author/critic. ILLUSTRATED.
$9.95

Colin Watson: SNOBBERY WITH VIOLENCE: CRIME STORIES
AND THEIR AUDIENCES
The noted mystery author examines the detective story and thriller
in sociological context. A classic of literary and social history.
ILLUSTRATED.
$8.95

To order by mail, simply send title and retail price, plus $3.00 for the first
book on any order and 50¢ for each additional book on that order, to
cover mailing and handling costs. New York State residents add applica-
ble sales tax. Enclose check or money order to: *Mysterious Press Mail
Order, 129 West 56th Street, New York, New York 10019.*